VIVEKANANDA

Speeches and Writings: A Critical Study

VIVEKANANDA

Speeches and Writings: A Critical Study

C.L. KHATRI

PRESTIGE

PRESTIGE BOOKS
3/28, East Patel Nagar
New Delhi 110 008

ISBN: 81-7551-086-2

Composed by Vivek Mathur, Delhi 110 006 Ph. 3981867
Printed by Chaman Offset Press, New Delhi 110 002

Contents

for

Late Professor Ramachandra Prasad

and

Sri Ram Jatan Lal Khatri

Preface

Books on Swami Vivekananda are legion. Since his death in 1902, each year produces an impressive daunting quota of books and articles, editions and casebooks, anniversary lectures, monographs, notes and dissertations. But these are concerned with the life, personality and philosophy of Vivekananda. There is no book available that deals exclusively with the literary value of his work and presents a critical assessment of Vivekananda as a Litterateur. *Chintanayak Vivekananda*, a comprehensive book in Bengali, deals with his poetry but even that is sketchy. The sheer bulk of his work in prose calls for the literary evaluation of his works which have hitherto remained neglected.

To write a book on one who wrote and spoke on all aspects of life, this world and the other world, and that too without any model, is an arduous task. I have tried my best to present Vivekananda as the poet, the writer, the orator and the philosopher. We find that his writings, speeches, letters and poems are all stamped with his idiosyncratic personality, and that his philosophy of Advaita Vedanta and Vedantic images knit them into a seamless garment and can be judged as a whole and regarded as constituting a single enormous volume

The first chapter, entitled "Introduction," centres round the personality and writings of Swami Vivekananda, a seminal mind in Indian-English literature and a trail-blazing propounder of the Advaita whose oratory shook the western world and drew the attention of his contemporaries towards a religion which most of the common readers in Europe and America considered abstruse and incomprehensively recondite.

The Life of Swami Vivekananda evaluates the formative influences on him and shows the evolution of a man and a saint rather than the emergence of a literary giant. Therefore, a revaluation of the formative influences on him from a literary perspective has been done in the second chapter.

The chapters concerning his oratory, poetry and prose style are comprehensive literary evaluation that establishes him as a prolific Indian-English writer and one of the pioneers of English prose and mystic poetry in India. The chapter "Prose Style" includes his letters also. It bears frequent references to his oratory, for his prose is basically rhetorical, but the chief concern is his written English that includes his three treatises: Bhakti-, Raja-and Karma-Yogas besides his articles and paper on "Hinduism."

"Philosophy," says Charles A. Moore, "to be philosophy must be universal. . . . Total truth is the life-blood of philosophy." Vivekananda's writings and speeches that run into nine volumes embody 'the total truth' and this is the life blood of his literature. In him philosophy and poetry shake hands and hence an attempt has been made in the chapter "Advaita Vedanta" to interpret the Upanishadic knowledge in the light of his own experiences.

In a work like the present one, the use of Sanskrit technical terms is inevitable, but care has been taken to explain them.

The writing of this book has put me under several happy obligations. First and foremost, I must record my indebtedness to Dr. Ashok Kumar who has been the cornerstone of this whole endeavour. I must take this occasion to pay my heart-felt homage to my mentor and preceptor late Dr. Ram Chandra Prasad. I have benefited from his lectures and comments. To my great distress he could not see the fruition of my endeavour.

I also wish to thank Dr. Bijay Bahadur Singh, Reader, Dept. of English, College of Commerce, Patna; Dr. Ramesh Chandra Prasad Sinha, Head Dept. of English, B.N. College, Pana; B.K. Tripathi, Reader, Dept. of English, A.N. College, Patna; Dr. Visvanath Chatterjee, Visiting Professor of English, Rabindra Bharati University, Calcutta; Prof. Shaileshwar Sati Prasad, Head, Dept of English. Science College, Patna and Prof. R.K. Dhawan, University of Delhi, whose comments inspired me to get it published.

I cannot help expressing my thankfulness to Swami Bodhasaranandaji of Advaita Ashrama, Swami Amaleshanandaji, the then librarian of Turiyananda Library, Ramakrishna Mission Ashrama, Patna, and to the President, Advaita Ashrama, Calcutta for giving written permission to quote from several books published by the Ashrama and to my friend Dr. Gajendra Kumar and Dr. Kumar Chandradeep, my younger brother Abhimanyu and my wife Seema Khatri who have always helped me in my literary pursuits.

Introduction

Swami Vivekananda was born in Calcutta on 12 January 1863 on Monday at 33 minutes 33 seconds past 6 a.m. on the auspicious occasion of *Makar Sankranti* in the family of Bhuvaneshwari and Vishwanath Datta.

As we know the family background has always been of prime importance in shaping the future of a child. Narendra's family, basically liberal and orthodox, was held in high esteem for its affluence, philanthropy, scholarship and learning. His father Vishwanath Datta, a man of learning and master of English and Persian literature, was attorney at law in the high court of Calcutta. He was proficient in Bengali, Hindi, English, Persian, Urdu, and Sanskrit. His mother Bhuvaneshwari Devi was a devout lady who prayed to Vireshwar Shiva at Varanasi for a son to carry on the family tradition, for she had only two daughters. It is assumed that Narendra, her eldest son, was the boon of Lord Shiva. So she named him Vireshwar whose nick-name was Bileh. Later he came to be called Narendranath or Naren. Subsequently, his parents were blessed with two more sons. In the physical, mental and spiritual power, he was exceptionally gifted. The popular but surprisingly anonymous book entitled *The Life of Swami Vivekananda by His Eastern and Western Disciples* portrays his childhood in these words:

> Narendranath was a naughty child, subject to fits of restlessness during which he was beyond control. At such times he would wear the family out. Bribes, threats, everything was tried—nothing was of any avail. Finally, Bhuvaneshwari found that if she poured cold water on the head of the scream-

> ing child, chanting the name of Shiva in his ears at the same time, or if she threatened him with, "Shiva will not let you go to Kailas if you do not behave," he would quiet down and become his eager joyous self again. (*Life*, I:12)

The power of meditation was inborn in him. He was able to plunge himself in meditation even at the age of eight. Many stories of his childhood that exhibit this quality in him can be found in his *Biography* by Nikhilananda and in his *Life by Eastern and Western Disciples.* Other tendencies of his childhood that have a bearing on his personality are his intense love for mendicants, ascetics and street singers, for pets and animals. He had a cow, a monkey, a goat, a peacock, pigeons and guinea pigs to play with and to love. He was compassionate to his friends, the poor and the needy. The quality of leadership and readiness to rise to the occasion can be traced to his childhood. He was friendly to his servants, the coachman and syce.

He was one with nature. His disciples believe that he was the incarnation of God Himself and put forward the unusual feature of Naren as proof of his enlightenment. Once Naren himself told one of his friends that as soon as drowsiness overtook him, a light of changing hues would appear between his eyebrows and would envelop his whole body with its bright radiance.

For his early education, his father and particularly his mother were very solicitous. His first guru (teacher) was his mother who used to tell him stories about gods and goddesses, Indian rishis and legendary heroes. It was a practice in the family to read out the *Ramayana*, the *Bhagavad Gita* and the *Mahabharata* to the boys and the ladies of the family at midday. His mother used to perform this task. She taught him Bengali alphabet and had always been a good guide to him. Whenever he had any problem, he rushed to his mother.

His formal education, however, began when he was six years old. He was admitted to a traditional school after performing *Khali Samskar*. But within a few days he was called back from the school as he was learning abusive words from his schoolmates. It was decided to have a private tutor at home. Thus he got his primary education at his worship-hall among his cousins and other boys.

His old relative, Nrisimha Datta, also contributed significantly to his education, besides his mother and his father. His father helped him become an accomplished singer and Nrisimha Datta, a learned man in Sanskrit lore, taught him the aphorisms of Sanskrit grammar *Mugdhabodha*. This training in Sanskrit in his boyhood helped him acquire a deeper and wider knowledge of Sanskrit literature. In this way, his schooling at home went for two years. In 1871, he was enrolled in the ninth class (equivalent to the present primary class two) at the Metropolitan Institution run by Pandit Ishwarchandra Vidyasagar. Here again he was unusually restless and felt it difficult to remain seated in the classroom. He frequently changed his position. His memory and intelligence were simply superb. He was able to reproduce the whole lesson taught to him. Romain Rolland writes that he remembered and stored in his memory what he once read. Such was his intelligence that the curriculum took little of his time and he was left with plenty of time and energy to carry out his extra curriculum activities. His favourite avocations were games and sports of several kinds, cooking, acting and singing songs in the temple. He was good at boxing, cricket, riding, swimming, racing and other sports. He was in the habit of learning one pastime after another. In the beginning, he was antipathetic to English language. But he realized its need and began to master it with a fervent zeal. And he did so in a very short time. An unmanageably naughty boy turned into an inexhaustible pursuer of learning. He was an avid reader of the books of history, philosophy, literature and religion. His quest for God became more fervent. His habit of getting lost in trance continued and his heart went on softening and broadening.

In 1877, his family shifted to Raipur for two years. There, he spent his time in an intimate contact with his father and his learned friends. In other words, he was placed in an atmosphere of maturity and scholarship taking him out of his boyish company. He experienced and realized a 'spiritual ecstasy' for the first time while travelling to Raipur in a cart. This imprinted an unforgettable mark on his mind. As he himself recalled: "What I saw and felt when going through the forest has for ever remained firmly imprinted in my memory." (*Life*, I:40) This incident worked as catalytic agent in accelerating his quest for truth, the ultimate reality. It was the period when he developed a keen sense of personal dignity; and when he returned to Calcutta, he was a transformed boy. He had developed a 'regal bearing' and a coterie of 'intellectual peers.' But his assiduous pursuit to knowledge continued. He mastered the game of chess. He learned to play on *Pakhawaj, Tabla, Esraj* and *Sitar* from the reputed masters like Beni Gupta, Ahmad Khan and Jagannath Mishra. He excelled his masters in vocal music. His voice was sweet, moving, melodious and intoxicating. In 1879, he got through the entrance examination and entered the First year Arts class in the Presidency College the following year. This was the next turning point in his life as he stepped into 'a world of new ideas and experiences.' In F.A. his subjects were English, History, Mathematics, Logic and Psychology. He passed the F.A. examination in the second division in 1881. He retained the same subjects in B.A. Examination except one change—Philosophy in place of Logic and Psychology. He graduated in 1884. He was a dedicated student of philosophy and literature and made 'great headway in the art of composition and rhetoric', and western philosophy and history of different nations. He was a genius and wizard of learning beyond comparison as the principal of the College William Hastie remarked: "Narendranath is really a genius. I have travelled far and wide but I have never yet come across a lad of his talents and possibilities, even in German Universities, amongst philosophical students. He is bound to make his mark in life!" (*Life*, I:48)

In these days, his mind underwent a psychological transformation. He became intensely analytical and 'subordinated imagination to the demands of reason' and subjected tradition, religion and beliefs to severe analysis; and he was leaning more towards God: "What shall learning be in the presence of the Lord." He drew aesthetic pleasure in devotional songs. He was not only a musician but also a 'theoretician' as is reflected in his first treatise *Sangita-Kalptaru* in Bengali (in 1887). Thus his formal education came to an end after graduation and a new intense spiritual education began under the leadership of Shri Ramakrishna Paramahansa—the Indian Swan.

He first came to know about Ramakrishna from Professor William Hastie who asked his students to see this man if they wanted to know what trance was. In November 1881, he first met Ramakrishna at the house of Shri Surendranath Mitra. After some time Narendra went along with his friends to Dakshineswar to see his Christ, Ramakrishna. Ramakrishna was in fact waiting for his St. Peter, the foremost apostle, to disseminate the results of his realization of Truth to the world. In Ramakrishna, the modern age has an answer to all the quarrels among different religions. He practised all religions and reached the same Truth, God. He saw Divine Mother even in his wife. In this meeting Naren swayed his master into ecstasy by the spiritual melody of his song.

> Let us go back once more, O mind, to our proper home!
> Here in this foreign land of earth
> Why should we wander aimlessly in stranger's guise?
> (Nikhilananda, 1987, 23)

This was not his own composition. It was the song used to be sung in Brahmo Samaj. At this age Naren, under the influence of science, had grown into a sceptic who wanted to achieve God if there is any, to verify everything himself. At first Naren held him as a mad man, when he called him the incarnation of *Narayana*. The whole attitude of Ramakrishna was beyond the comprehension of Narendra. He put forth his favourite question: "Have you seen God?" The reply quenched his thirst as Narendra used to recall: "Yes, I see Him just as I see you here, only in a much intenser sense," he went on: "one can see and talk to Him as I am seeing and talking to you." (*Life*, 77)

At that time he thought of Ramakrishna as 'monomaniac,' yet 'the holiest of the holy, a true saint.' And he continued to visit him even when he was in great distress. While he was graduating, he met with Job's fate. Like Job (in *The Book of Job*) he was stripped of all fortune. His father suddenly died and left the family burdened with a heavy debt as he had lived beyond his means. To add to his grief, creditors, like hungry wolves, began to prowl about the door and his relatives brought a title suit for the partition of the ancestral home. The responsibility of the family fell on his shoulders, and he wandered about to find a job but in vain. Friends turned into foes and well-wishers slammed their doors in his face.

Such an inhuman treatment he received that he doubted, like Job, the Divine providence and thought "if the world were a handiwork of the Devil." His friends and some of the devotees of the Master ascribed to him many filthy crimes, which he had supposedly committed. Narendra was greatly mortified to know all this. Here also, the protagonist was comforted by God and was doubly rewarded. He won the case, got a job in a school though he gave it up soon. His family's economic condition improved a lot and he could renounce the worldly life and become a Sannyasi. He foiled every attempt of his family to get him married and remained a devout bachelor.

He was privileged to sit at the lotus feet of his Master for about five years. He, along with other disciples, nursed the ailing master at a garden house at Cossipore day and night. Realizing the approaching end of his mortal existence, the Master appointed Narendra the leader of his disciples and his spiritual heir. He transmitted his whole spiritual power to Narendra to enable him to accomplish the task assigned to him by the Mother. On August 16, 1886, he entered into *Nirvikalp Samadhi*. Though he cast off his physical body, it is believed, his apparition appeared many times to help them or to instruct them.

Narendra could no longer perform his duty as their leader because an intense inner conflict within him was going on. On the one hand he found it difficult to run the Barangore monastery while on the other hand his heart hankered for a wandering life. He did not want his brother disciples to be the traditional ascetics in solitary caves. They should rather broaden their outlook by assimilating the thought-currents of the world. They should actively live in the world but renounce the worldliness of life. They took a vow of celibacy and poverty. Having made some temporary excursions, he set out for the intensive tour of India in 1890. He travelled far and wide, lived among kings and pariahs. But he failed to make a mark on the society until his genius was recognized by America. It was America which recognized his talent and highlighted it before the world and India as well. Indians celebrated his victory at the Parliament of Religions in 1893. From the Parliament, he became known by the new name Swami Vivekananda that was given to him by the King of Khetri on his departure for America.

In fact his literary contribution began with his address at the Parliament of Religionss, Chicago. Here, for the first time, all his speeches were recorded and noted down. He delivered twelve lectures at the plenary sessions of the Parliament and at the scientific section, an affiliated unit of it. Most of these lectures were not written. But he wrote himself a paper on Hinduism and read it at the Parliament and it proved to be an epoch-making one. During this course, the Swami became intimate with a number of scholars and persons of repute and influenced them immensely. He and his disciples attributed it to the divine providence. Among the influenced persons, the noble ones are Professor John Henry Wright and his wife, Merwin-Marie Snell, the President of the scientific section, Mrs George W. Hale and others. Though Hinduism was introduced to America by Emerson and others much before Vivekananda, it was rather a poor and ill representation. Among the audience, very few knew anything substantial of the Hindu religion. Therefore the credit goes to Vivekananda for impregnating the mind and heart of the American with the crystal thoughts and living pictures of the Universal Religion—the Hinduism. This oriental scholar left a lasting impression on the minds of "the hundreds of enlightened and liberal-minded persons. Emersonians, Transcendentalists, Neochristians, Theosophists, Universalists, Congregationalists." (*Life*, 429) Some of his acquaintances became his disciples and embraced Hinduism while others worshipped and adored him remaining in their homes. As far as American influence upon him is concerned, Romain Rolland maintains that he was conversant with the thoughts of the Anglo-Saxon fore-runners of the spirit of Asia, Emerson, Thoreau and Walt Whitman. They were the persons who kept the Hindu thought alive in America.

After the parliament, Swami Vivekananda undertook a series of 'apostolic campaigns' to spread the message of Shri Ramakrishna. In the beginning, he entered into contract with a lecture bureau. In 1894, he broke this contract and organized free courses in Oriental learning in a rented room. There he took up his ambitious project of writing a treatiese on Raja-Yoga. Around June 1895, he finished this book with the help of his amanuensis Miss S.E. Waldo (afterwards Sister Haridas). The book entitled *The Philosophy of Yoga* (Raja-Yoga) was published from New York in

1896. This was the first book published in his lifetime and at once brought him fame and name in the literary world. The great Russian novelist Leo Tolstoy, Indologist Max Mueller and philosopher William James were greatly impressed with this accomplished work of art. This work alone is sufficient to establish him as a writer. He dictated two more treatises on *Bhakti-Yoga* and *Karma-Yoga*. *Jnana-Yoga* comprises his lectures delivered in London and America.

From America, he went to England in December 1895. But England won the heart of the conqueror of America as he asserted: "No one ever landed on English soil with more hatred in his heart for a race than I did for the English. . . . There is none among you. . . . who loves the English people more than I do now." He was immensely influenced by the masters of Indology, Max Mueller and Paul Deussen whom he met. The young Swami of India bowed before the old Sage of Europe (Max Mueller) and hailed him as a spirit of his race, the reincarnation of an ancient Rishi.

In America and Europe he travelled a lot, visited numerous cities, villages and important places; and met and talked to many dignitaries and commoners. A lovely and picturesque account of all this can be found in Marie Louise Burke's *Swami Vivekananda in the West: New Discoveries*. The great warrior of India, having taken the world by storm, returned to his motherland on 15th January 1897 where the jubilant countrymen passionately waited to bathe him in the heartiest welcome. But this whirlwind tour of the West had exhumed the vitals of his body. Thereafter, he remained constantly ill. The people in India were jubilant at his success but he was weeping because all his glory and 'treasures of soul' could not provide him 'three hundred million rupees necessary for his dream of the material regeneration of India.' Here again, the saviour of India was not to rest. He once again crossed the land from the South to the North. Wherever he went and whenever he spoke, he made people delirious, threw them into a state of ecstasy. The immediate need was to establish a machinery with dedicated soldiers and rich funds. He knew that if India wants economic development, she has to harness her own resources and has not to stretch her arms for alms. He started the publication of three magazines—*Prabudha Bharata* in English, *Udbodhan* and *Brahmavadin* in Bengali. On May 1, 1897, he founded the Ramakrishna Mission in his presidentship as 'a servant of the Master.' The organization was based on dictatorship because the time was not ripe for a democratic system. He was in a hurry and wanted pragmatic results. The mission's work was in full swing. Sister Nivedita actively participated in the relief work during an epidemic or famine. A great monastery was built at Belur.

In June 1899, Swami Vivekananda set out upon his second journey to the West. After a brief stay at London, he left for America where he had founded a Vedantic centre. Swami Abhedananda was looking after it in his absence. He founded new Vedantic centres at San Francisco, Okland and Alamada. At Santa Clara, he built an Ashrama on the sixty acres of land offered to him. Turiyananda was deputed there to train the western disciples and students in monastic life. He had delivered numerous lectures during this period. Some are published in *Complete Works of Swami Vivekananda* but most of them remained unwritten in the absence of a second Goodwin, his secretary during his first visit. He visited Paris, Berlin, Austria, Greece, Cairo and other places. In December 1900, he returned to India and was shocked to know about the demise of Mr. Sevier at Mayavati Ashrama. He rushed to the Ashrama despite his decaying health because of asthma and deep exhaustion. But he was happy to see the work accomplished there. He celebrated his thirty-eighth birthday on January 12, 1901 and said: 'My body is done for.' He was conscious of his approaching death. After celebrating his birthday, he came to Belur Math on January 24. He travelled with his mother to the holy places of Eastern Bengal, Assam, Dacca and Shillong for the last time. On his return to Belur, he found himself almost dead, lying on death-bed. Yet he was so kind-hearted and forthcoming that he set out for Bodh-Gaya on the request of a Japanese visitor Okakura but he could go only up to Varanasi where he fainted and was brought back to Belur. He achieved *Mahanirvan* on 4th July 1902. But he had nothing to repent for his departure at the age of thirty-nine, as he said: "I have done enough for fifteen hundred years."

Swami Vivekananda returned to his eternal abode. But what did he leave behind him? How did the present generation come to know him and draw inspiration from him? Certainly he left behind him trail-blazing thoughts through his works that are still very popular in India and abroad. The world in general and India in particular are indebted to him for leaving behind the train of comrades dedicated to the cause of nation and humanity. Though K.R. Srinivasa Iyengar does not properly assess his contribution to Indian-English literature in his book *Indian Writing in English*, he wishes to cherish his work as 'National literature.'

Swami Vivekananda's writings and speeches that run into nine volumes have attracted hundreds of reviews. A number of books have been written on his thought, his philosophy of Vedanta and on his life. Thousands of lectures have been delivered on his centenary and anniversary all over the world. Russia and America besides India have shown special interest in him. In all these works two points have been predominant: his life and his philosophy. These are preoccupied with what he said rather than how he said it. This is, however, by no means intended to refute the importance of such works. But at the same time one is reminded of what T.S. Eliot insisted upon—that meaning was an element of form, that a work of art should be judged by how it is said and not by what is said. For the literature written by Vivekananda, one can neither ignore 'what is said' nor 'how it is said.' Both must be taken together. This book is an attempt in that direction with all humility and with gratitude to those who have written and made significant research on him, particularly to Romain Rolland for his *The Life of Vivekananda and the Universal Gospel*, to his eastern and western disciples for *The Life of Swami Vivekananda*, to Nikhilananda for *Vivekananda: A Biography*, to the President Shri Ramakrishna Math, Madras for *Facets of Vivekananda*, to Marie Louise Burke for her outstanding research work *Swami Vivekananda in the West—New Discoveries* (Six Volumes), to Swami Abhedananda for his *Vivekananda and His Work*.

Though Romain Rolland cannot claim to be a detached observer, he tried his best to be objective in dealing with Swami Vivekananda and his works. Though he presents a graphic picture of his life and message, he leaves out the account of his childhood and the family. He deals with his works in the latter part of the book, but does not assess his literary contribution. On this account one cannot accuse him nor can one underestimate the significance of his work. This is perhaps the only popular book on him that ventured upon making comparisons with other poets, musicians and writers. "Vivekananda's words are great music, phrases in the style of Beethoven, stirring rhythms like the march of Handel Choruses." (1988) Swamiji's works remind him over and over again of Beethoven.

Again in the chapter "America at the Time of Vivekananda's First Visit," he gives a brilliant account of the thoughts of Emerson, Thoreau, Walt Whitman and the contemporary literary scene. He took up the stupendous task of measuring 'how far the American spirit had been impregnated' by the 'Hindu thought in the 19th century.' The account of Walt Whitman's poetry and his thoughts and the influence of the Hindu philosophy on his works is elucidated and presented with several quotations from his poetry that justify his claim. However, he exhausts his energy in proving how Swamiji came to know him or met his intimate ones rather than showing the meeting points of the poetry of the two poets. He deals with his philosophy of four yogas in the chapter "Great Path" but remains silent about his poetry. In *The Life of Vivekananda* (one of the earliest biographies of Swamiji written in 1931), Romain Rolland's pregnancy of imagination and elegance of language place him high in the ranks of litterateurs. He writes about three subjects—pseudo-vedantism in the contemporary America, his Gospel and then the sketch of Ramakrishna Math and Mission and of the relation between 'Hellenic-Christian mysticism' and 'Hindu mysticism.' His objective was to introduce Vivekananda to his French and other European readers. He has paved way for further study by hinting at certain aspects that had hitherto remained unnoticed by his other biographers.

The life of Swami Vivekananda is the field in which a great deal of research has been conducted. Among the biographies, *The Life of Swami Vivekananda* by his disciples and *Vivekananda: A Biography* are two major books in English. The latter is but a sort of abridged edition of the former, a medium sized biography. But the source of dates of the two seems to be different for there is difference in the years mentioned by the two books about when Swami Vivekananda was enrolled in the Metropolitan Institution. Nikhilananda gives the year 1870 while his disciples mention it as 1871. From here onwards the two maintain one year difference in all accounts which should have been rectified, since the two are published from the same house. However, Ramakrishna Ashrama holds *The Life* as more authentic. *The Life* was first published in July 1912 and has been updated in every further edition. However, a biography cannot have the same fervour, the same personal touch that an autobiography has. But Swamiji had neither the time nor the desire to write his autobiography. Human mind is so subtle and complex that it often becomes difficult for the person himself to express in words what he really feels. Another problem is that a biography is attempted in the last phase of one's life or after one's death. We very often do not possess the written account of that period of life when the person has not become famous .Therefore, *The Life*, however comprehensive, is not complete. There are still a few chapters in his life which are not covered in the book. One such chapter has been dealt with by Beni Shanker Sharma in his book, *Swami Vivekananda: A Forgotten Chapter of His life.* Nevertheless the authors have spared no pains in procuring all facts about his life from whatever sources possible and in incorporating published and unpublished materials about his life. It is certainly the best of all available biographies.

However, the book contains some anomalies. For example, there is difficulty in understanding whether Narendranath was the youngest child. If not (he was followed by two more brothers) then they should have referred to at least their birth and name. A casual reader may fall into the delusion that Naren was the youngest child as it reads: "Though she had been blessed with motherhood at an early age, her first child, a son, and her second, a daughter, had died in their childhood. Her next three children were all daughters." (*Life*, 10) And later it is written, "in due course a son was born to her." (*Life*, 10) A reader is not expected to go through the whole of the book to know how many brothers and sisters he had.

Naren renounced his home in 1886. It means that he lived with his family for about twenty three years. And we have no account of his interaction with his brothers, virtually nothing of the two brothers, as if they were non-existent. They only figure as liability on Naren after the death of his father: "The body of his father lay ready to be taken to the burning-ghat on funeral cot. His mother, two young brothers and sisters were weeping and wailing." (*Life*, 120)

The Life does not present the chronicle account of Swami Vivekananda's writings. He is said to be a prolific writer of Bengali and English. *The Life* presents the development of the man but not of the artist. The two, however, should not be discussed in isolation from each other. Again, the authors of *The Life* proclaim him a 'great' Bengali writer but make scanty reference to his Bengali works and do not bother to prove how he was a great writer. A thorough reading of the book shows us that it is more the biography of a religious-preacher and a reformer rather than of a writer. It is by no means the life of the poet or the artist, that one finds in *The Lives of the English Poets* by Samuel Johnson. One feels compelled to say that his disciples have failed to do justice with Swami Vivekananda, the writer. The book does refer to his four treatises on Karma-Yoga, Bhakti-Yoga, Raja-Yoga and Jnana-Yoga. But when he took up writing a particular book and when he finished it, when that was published and how that was written are not dealt with. The four treatises are dealt with in just one paragraph:

> By this time the Swami had concluded his lectures on Karma-Yoga, Raja-Yoga, Bhakti-Yoga and Jnana-Yoga. The first two of these class-series were, by the labours of Mr. Goodwin, ready for publication and were shortly to come out in book form constituting two of the Swami's great works, *Karma-Yoga* and *Raja-Yoga*. On the whole, the American journals received and reviewed these books favourably and they attained a wide circulation, *Raja-Yoga* arousing considerable discussion among the psychologists and physiologists of some of the leading Universities. *Bhakti-Yoga* was soon to be published in India, and, in addition, several of the Swami's Sunday lectures, which are later to form a part of this book *Jnana-Yoga*, had already appeared in pamphlet form. (*Life*, II:70)

And of course a casual reference here and there can be seen; but there is no systematic elucidation of these classics. Interestingly enough, Romain Rolland has done justice with these classics in the chapter "The Great Paths." His other activities and developments like his addresses before and after the parliament, his monastic and teaching work in America and England, his tour of India and the west and matha's activities are vividly presented in the two volumes.

Another monumental research work carried out by Marie Louise Burke was first published in three volumes. titled *Swami Vivekananda in the West: New Discoveries* and subtitled *His Prophetic Mission* part one and part two; *The World Teacher* part one and part two; *A New Gospel* part one and part two. It is not merely a biography of Swamiji in the West, but an encyclopedic book that gives us most comprehensive records about Swamiji in the West. The inclusion of unpublished letters and newspaper reports is of immense value to the readers and researchers on Vivekananda as they throw light on his personality. The author has well presented new materials against historical background, the picture of his antagonists, the historical background of the Parliament of Religions. The controversy between him and his opponents P.C. Mazumdar, Theosophist and Christian Missionaries and again between him and Pandit Ramabai are well related. A chronology of his work published in the Appendix of volumes two and three is of particular interest to the students of literature. The role played by Swami Vivekananda in the Parliament of Religions has been discussed not in isolation but in the light of the activities and speeches of other speakers. In other words the whole scene has been presented. Records of reaction (for and against) to his speeches have been exhibited photographically. But at times they appear as loose mosaic patch-works as Marie Louise Burke embarks upon accommodating almost all newly available reports on him and on his writings and speeches. In all such evaluations of his speeches and writings, the most obvious lack is the approach of literary criticism. Most of the quoted news reports, though of interest, are repetitious and of general journalistic nature. For example, she quotes from *Chicago Inter Ocean* of September 1894: "There was no delegate to the Parliament of Religionss who attracted more courteous attention in Chicago by his winning ways, his ability, and his fearless discussion of all questions relating to his religion than Swami Vivekananda who represented the Hindoos of South India." (I:188)

Again she quotes from *Li Hung Chang's Scrap-Book*: "When, however, Vivekananda spoke, they saw that they had a Napoleon to deal with. His first speech was no less than a revelation." (I, 139)

There are numerous quotations like these, at times they mispresent Swamiji's mission as in the former quotation it is erroneous to say that he "represented the Hindoos of South India." For the literary criticism, such quotations serve the purpose to show how his English was accepted and recognized by America and England. Articles on the Swami's writings and speeches tend to adopt a philosophical line of criticism. One may ponder for a while why has no literary attention been paid to his classics in the articles published during those days. A plausible reason can be the euphoria created by his philosophy among the western people. The people concerned were either obsessed with his teachings or antagonistic to him. And he was looked at from that point of view—as a moral teacher. monk and philosopher. Another reason can be his unattachment to the claim of his being a creative artist or litterateur. He was a Sannyasi unattached to worldly achievements for himself. How could he have claimed for it? In chapter 13 of Vol. 1, Part II she presents his gestures and gives ample proof of further literary attention over his speeches and writing. Marie Louise in Author's *Note* to the book claims to have given "New interpretations, based on new findings and also on a reexamination of the Swami's published letters and other writings." In volume II Part I subtitled 'The World Teacher,' she proceeds along the chronological line, citing extensively from his letters, news reports. articles and lectures. She tells how he was anxious to write books of *Karma-Yoga, Bhakti-Yoga, Raja-Yoga* and *Jnana-Yoga*. In the chapter 'New York, December 1895' and 'New York: January, February 1896' she deals with his four classics *Karma-Yoga, Bhakti-Yoga, Raja-Yoga* and *The Science and Philosophy of Religion* which constituted his lectures on *Jnana-Yoga*. But the author is concerned with 'The Teacher' and not with the writer—the aforesaid chapters centre round his teachings and philosophy. No attempt has been made to see his works from literary point of view. The author has asserted at some places that Swamiji was a poet and writer but does not go along with it.

However. one cannot help wondering if his books are literary productions. What about his poems? Can he be called a poet? There is a plethora of related questions as David Daiches points out in his *Critical Approaches to Literature*.

> Not only 'How good is this work and why?' and 'How do we differentiate between the good and the less good?' are the subjects for debate, but such matters are discussed as the relation between works of literature and other phases of culture, psychological questions concerning the way the creative writer operates, sociological questions about the way in which his place in society affects his way of writing, semantic questions about what happens to language when it is employed in a certain way, his literary conventions, his ideas, textual and bibliographical inquiries. (175)

The writers on Swami Vivekananda are silent on these questions and the like. The present book aims to fill this gap and assess his literary contribution.

Formative Influences

The influences that worked upon this trail blazing propounder of Advaita, Swami Vivekananda have been the subject of interest to his biographers (His Eastern and Western Disciples). But what were the formative influences upon this seminal mind in Indian-English literature? Perhaps it is the subject that eludes his disciples, and they have to be content with referring to some books of English literature he had studied. However, we cannot segregate the development of a Sannyasi and that of a writer. It is scarcely thinkable that the revolutions in his life, thought and feelings that we have referred to in the preceding chapter should not have left their mark on his work. His work draws much of its characteristic strength from deeply felt private experiences and preoccupations. It is, therefore, important to see the factors that forged to evolve Narendra into a divine Mahatma; and the direct or indirect influences that developed his art of writing. Swami Ranganathananda in one of his lectures at Moscow University entitled "Swami Vivekananda. His Humanism," listed the influences on him in this way:

> These influences were four: first, his assimilation of the rich spiritual element of Indian culture in his early life through the informal education received from his mother and from his own studies; second, his assimilation of the energy and spirit of Western culture through his formal modern education in school and college as a youth; third, his silent spiritual training under his Guru', Shri Ramakrishna, . . . And fourth, his intimate acquaintance through his extensive travels. (25)

The obvious limitation is of its being generic in nature and few points need to be added. One cannot afford to overlook hereditary influences, the influence of the Brahmo Samaj and some other influences. Again, it was not only 'the spiritual elements of Indian culture' that he assimilated but had become one with the sufferings and miseries of the Indian masses and wished to be born again and again and to bear thousands of miseries. His disciples deal with these influences elaborately and vividly in the chapter "The Man in the Making" of *The Life*: "A survey of Naren's youth shows three factors shaping his character and destiny: his innate spiritual tendency; . . . the influence of his family and of his studies; and thirdly, the guidance of his spiritual teacher Shri Ramakrishna, who raised him from the mire of unhappiness and scepticism to certainty and peace."

Having gone through his life and his works, we come to the conclusion that the influences that worked upon him to shape him into the sage of the century and pioneer of Indian-English literature are hereditary influences, his family and local surroundings, institutions and individuals, particularly Shri Ramakrishna, academic and literary influences, extensive tour of India and the influence of the West and his days of trials and tribulations.

Genetic or hereditary influence on the mind and body of a man is a scientifically established fact. Genes of parents and ancestors play a vital role in shaping the personality of a man. In Swami Vivekananda, these were too obvious and too intense to ignore. These not only shaped his body and mind but also determined his destiny. As a matter of fact, his grandfather had renunciated the world at the age of twenty five and become a monk in search of God. Vivekananda may not be the reincarnation of his grandfather, but certainly he inherited the seeds of monkhood and spiritual life that were developed by the recurrent projection of the same image, frequent visit of monks to him and by the stories of the renunciators and mystics. He had the athletic body of his father and sharp memory of his mother. There was a confluence in him of such feminine qualities as beauty, sweetness, softness and humility, and of such manly qualities as courage, restlessness and devil-dare. He inherited a great treasure of potential energy and the seeds of meditation. As he himself once narrated it to Mr. E.T. Sturdy (his English disciple): "Well, Sturdy, in my childhood I used to observe an inexhaustible force arising in me, overflowing my body, as it were. I used to become restless and could not keep quiet. This was why I used to fidget all the time. (*Life*, I, 32)

He had not acquired such qualities but had moulded them in the chosen direction and succeeded. Ramakrishna said that he was perfect by birth. Whether it is true or not is difficult to confirm. Another inborn spiritual quality was what he himself narrates:

> Whenever I came in contact with a particular object, man or place, it would sometimes appear to me as if I had been acquainted with it beforehand. But all my efforts to recollect were unsuccessful, and yet the impression persisted. . . . Later on I thought that it might be due to the law of transmigration. But soon I decided that such definite conclusions on the subject were not reasonable. Now I believe that before I was born I must have had visions somehow, of those subjects and people with whom I would have to come in contact in my present birth. Such memories have come every now and then throughout my life. (*Life*, I, 40-41)

We have no reason to doubt his contention but he himself is not very precise about the source of such memories. It is difficult to believe that his case is identical to that of Abhimanyu in the *Mahabharata*. However the influence of family atmosphere, of the relation between mother and father and of mother's physical and psychological condition on the developing child in the womb is undisputed. The child in the womb receives something more than mere food and water.

The society which includes local environment plays an important role in the development of a child. Vivekananda, as we have seen before, was born and brought up amidst the chanting of mantras, ringing of temple bells and the burning of incense. We have already seen that he was influenced by the charity of the family, prayer, visits of the wandering monks and sadhus, the recitation of the *Mahabharata* and the *Ramayana*. Among the earliest formative influences on Swami Vivekananda, it is said that his father shared with him his love for the *Bible* and the Persian mystics, while his mother undoubtedly taught him the oral traditions of Hinduism, the story of Nachiketa from the *Katha Upanishad*. It would be apt to recall that there were three streams of thought running in India; and Bengal was the seat of all. These were: Hindu thought, Muslim thought and Christian thought. Being a Hindu, Vivekananda was bathed in Hindu thought, culture and rituals. Since the Muslims had become Indian, the two could not live apart without being influenced by each other. A sort of mixed culture (Indo-Islamic) had developed at that time. Vivekananda learnt the art of *Lathi* and music from his Muslim teachers. When he entered Presidency College, he came in direct contact with the Christian ethos. In him, the three streams merged into one.

Vivekananda studied the philosophy of J.S. Hill, Kant, Hegel, Carlyle, Aristotle, Plato and Socrates and the history of Europe. He became conversant with the Greek and the Roman art, culture and literature and was influenced by the Renaissance and Reform movements. And in due course of time, he became the torch bearer of Indian Renaissance.

The Brahmo Samaj was the first reformative institution on which he pinned his hope for its activities were dynamic as against the demode and caducous state of Hindu society. It was a protestant movement against certain 'tenets of orthodox Hinduism.' He joined the Brahmo Samaj when he was a high school student. In him it aroused 'a tumult of thought and feeling,' and he was imbued with its ideas. He no more believed in polytheism and image worship. This print on his mind, however, evaporated when he met Ramakrishna. Influenced by Keshub Chunder Sen, he tried to imbibe his qualities—power of thought, depth of feeling, enthusiasm and 'personal magnetism.' He was not content with passivity as his disciples record that "he wanted to know the 'why' and 'how' of every phenomenon, mental or spiritual."

The influence of his father, his mother and his relatives on him are too obvious. His father helped him become an accomplished singer and Nrisimha Datta taught him the 'aphorisms of Sanskrit grammar *Mugdhabodha*. His mother told him: "Always be a man, my son!" Another maxim he was told by his mother was: "if you are right, stick to your guns, dead or alive." His father's laconical advice of good manners was "Never show surprise." The intent was to remain constantly unattached in both happiness and misery, castles and hovels. And to quote his words of gratitude: "I am indebted to my mother for the efflorescence of my knowledge." The above-mentioned influences are common in everyman's life. The greatest influence, however, came from Ramakrishna to whom Swamiji owed whatsoever he had.

The training of Vivekananda at the hands of Shri Ramakrishna, by which the young dynamic intellectual became a man-God, one who saw God in himself and in all beings, one who became like his master universal in his sympathy for man, is a momentous chapter in modern history with great consequences for the future.

Such was the influence of Ramakrishna on him that Swami Turiyananda said that Swamiji did not preach even a single idea of his own. Therefore a suggestion is made to think of the two in terms of one entity. Tapash Sankar Dutta in his *Study of Philosophy of Vivekananda* maintains that Ramakrishna is like an ocean when it is calm. Swami Vivekananda is the 'ocean lashed into waves.'

We may recall that it was Ramakrishna 'who transformed Narendra, a sceptic into a *Rishi*, and placed him next to Sankar in the hierarchy of the propounders of the Advaita. It was Ramakrishna who gave him the concept of the universality of religion, the oneness of soul (*Siva* as *Jiva*), the divinity of man. The life of Shri Ramakrishna illustrates the variety of processes open to individuals for the realization of their spiritual aspirations. He explored for humanity all the approaches to the realm of eternal wisdom, for there was no religious faith that he did not practise and no truth that he did not realize in his own life. His life is as such a bold and triumphant ascent from the level of dualistic worship to the height of absolutism through graded rungs of spiritual experiences. He has verified in his life that the three great orders of metaphysical thought—dualism, modified monism and absolute monism—are stages on the way to the Supreme Truth. They are not contradictory but, when added the one to the other, are complementary.

Swamiji expressed his indebtedness to his Master in these words: "I through the grace of God had the great good fortune to sit at the feet of one whose whole life was such an interpretation, whose life a thousand fold more than whose teaching was, a living commentary on the texts of the *Upanishads* was in fact the spirit of the Upanishads having in a human form," (*Works*, I, 542) In another context, he said:

> Without studying Ramakrishna Paramahansa first, one can never understand the real impact of the *Vedas*, the *Vedanta*, of the *Bhagavata* and the other *Puranas*. His life is a search-light of infinite power thrown upon the whole mass of Indian religious thought. He was the living commentary to the Vedas and to (sic) their aim. He had lived in one life the whole cycle of the national religious existence in India. (*Life*, I, 542)

He did not owe much to Indian-English prose writers of his time for his phraseology and language. Rather he owed much to a practically illiterate man Ramakrishna, for a readymade reservoir of phraseology with connotative significance, such as 'Mother,' 'Kali,' 'Lila' and 'Sakti,' and parables. He attributes the simplicity of his language and his colloquial style to his master in one of his letters. His master spoke with utter simplicity; the clarity, the concreteness and the accuracy of his style in which he has succeeded to illustrate the complex and abstract philosophies of Vedanta owe much to his clarity of vision and this clarity of vision is imparted to him by Shri Ramakrishna. Without a clear concept of a subject, one can neither speak convincingly nor write smoothly.

Some other personalities who influenced him are Pavhari Baba and Pramadadas Mitra. It is said that he remained under the spell of the former until the spirit of Ramakrishna intervened and brought him to his fold. He was charmed by his exceptional practice of Hatha-Yoga. Pramadadas Mitra, an eminent scholar of his time, was his friend. Just as Wordsworth got a lesson from an ordinary reaper, Vivekananda was taught a lesson by an ordinary 'nautch-girl' at the court of the king of Khetri, when he refused to enjoy her song and dance that she was performing at his court. She instantly sang a song:

> O Lord look not upon my evil qualities.
> Thy Name, O Lord, is Same-Sighted.
> One piece of iron is in the image in the temple,
> And another, the knife in the hand of the butcher;

> But when they touch the philosopher's stone,
> Both alike turn to gold. (*Life*, I, 286)

Such minor incidents helped him shake off his fanaticism and become 'same sighted' in the true sense of the term.

Another source of influence that was next to the *Gita* was the *Imitation of Christ* by Thomas a Kempis. He used to keep the *Gita* and the *Imitation of Christ* always with him and distributed hundreds of copies of these two. While mailing a copy of the *Imitation of Christ* to Pramadadas Mitra on 7 August, 1889, he wrote: "It is a wonderful book. One is astonished to find that such renunciation, Vairagya and Dasya-Bhakti have existed even among the Christians." (*Life*, I) From this letter we come to learn that Swamiji at that time of his life found in the pages of it a confirmation of Ramakrishna's teachings as well as a personal solace.

He was so much interested in this book that he published a selection from the *Imitation of Christ* with parallel passages from the Hindu scriptures and a preface to it in 1889 in *Sahitya Kalpadruma* (now a defunct magazine). He writes in its preface:

> *The Imitation of Christ* is a cherished treasure of the Christian world. This great book was written by a Roman Catholic Monk. . . . It would be more appropriate to say that each letter of the book is marked deep with the heart's blood of the great soul who had renounced all for his love of Christ. That great soul whose words, living and burning, have cast such a spell for the last four hundred years over the hearts of myriads of men and women; whose influence today remains as strong as ever and is destined to endure for all time to come. (*Works*, 8:159)

His intensive study of the *Bible* and the *Imitation of Christ* enriched his language by providing a rich treasure of Biblical images to use at his will. We may recall how Biblical images are the common features in the writings of the English and the Americans. In Swamiji we find both Vedantic and Biblical idioms frequently used. Jeane Machphail in his article 'The Imitation of Christ. In the Formative Years of Swami Vivekananda' points out one such symbol:

"He had apparently found a meaningful symbol in the Christian idea of the cross, representing as it does, total self-denial and acceptance of the Divine Will." (*Prabudha Bharata*, Aug. 1982) The author goes on to say that his interest in this book was further illustrated in his lecture *Practical Vedanta*. He uses, there, the authority of Thomas a Kempis to underscore his thesis that, while intellect is necessary to check errors, 'the real help is feeling love.'

There are many such terms that occur in his works, for example, the symbol of 'Medona,' 'deluge,' 'word,' 'Christ,' 'Darkness,' 'Helen,' 'Lamb,' etc. But they are replete largely with Vedantic idioms.

There are two basic factors that make a writer and an artist: inborn talent and training and practice. Intuition and inspiration that the Romanticists stressed, or what D.H. Lawrence said 'the wind that blows through me,' the supersensitivity and the chastity that Milton advocated as the prerequisite for a poet are things that the artist inherits. No amount of training can make these attainable. A man may be a good orator or a painter or a musician or for that matter any artist but he cannot be 'a lion among the deer' without being an inborn genius. So one can be an orator by birth or by practice. In Swamiji both factors merged together to produce a 'divine orator' and preacher whose oratory shook the West and awoke the East from its long stupor. Oratory was latent in him, practice and circumstances only manifested it powerfully.

Vivekananda inherited more than the power of intuition and meditation. He got an awakened *Kundalini* (Serpentine power) by birth. It is commonly believed in the Hindu religion that once the *Kundalini* is awakened, the door to infinite knowledge is opened; and the man becomes illumined like a god. He achieves a deep penetrating insight into the matter. This can be the supreme power in an artist that one can hopefully wish for though one hardly, if ever, achieves it. Swamiji is believed to have received an incessant flow of inspiration from beyond the state of reason more profound than what Wordsworth or Shelley had received. Where does it come from? It comes from instinct and develops into reason and reason into transcendental consciousness. Commonly, a writer comes to the state of reason and at best intuition and not beyond that. In this respect, he outshines other professional writers. Keats and

Shelley, the champions of inspirational poetry failed to see the unity among the three states of mind.

The pivotal question is the enquiry into the factors that developed, shaped and influenced his skill of writing, composing verse, translating, delivering lectures. Since he had neither any formal training in the art of writing nor a litterateur's family background, nor Indian-English literature had taken any concrete shape at that time, he had to depend much on his reading of the Western English books and the general education that he had received at college to give language to his thought. The literature of the time was actuated by the social, political and religious milieu of the time. The volatile milieu gave birth to more lecturing, pamphleteering and journalism than to literary pursuit. Since there has not been any systematic study of the literary influences on Vivekananda who was reticent about it, we have to depend on his works and his *Life*. By way of comparing his language, style and technique with others, one can deduce some influences that would have worked upon him.

Before being a writer of any genre, Vivekananda was an orator. The source of his oratory does not lie at any one point. It can be traced to his boyhood when he was a leader among his friends; a lion among his school and college fellows. This leadership quality was inborn in him. A leader has to be talkative, persuasive and imposing. It is a psychological fact that a man's future is shaped in his boyhood and the teacher of the school leaves the deepest imprint on his mind. It was the privilege of Narendra to be a student of Pandit Ishwarchandra Vidyasagar, a scholar of English and a proficient speaker.

No less important was the environment of his home. His father, a great lawyer, was the king among men and professionally expert in oratory. Religious preachers, monks and lawyers used to visit his home and their talk appealed to him and inspired him. His formal training in the art of singing and music went a long way in honing his oratory.

Above all, the whole atmosphere in India was charged with a rebellious spirit and reform movement that gave birth to a number of orators. Naren had the opportunity to listen to them and to imbibe their art. He used to deliver speeches at school and college.

At one occasion in Metropolitan Institution, he spoke for half an hour before Surendra Nath Banerjee. the greatest orator of that time. and moved him by the magic of his speech. Again, Brahmo Samaj that could boast of having such powerful orators as Raja Ram Mohun Roy and Keshub Chander Sen imparted him practical training in that field. Gradually he learnt the art of catching the nerve of the audience, to shift the tone and subject according to the place and the audience. His rich knowledge backed him in this art.

Trial and error method also helped him a lot. Before going to Chicago, he traversed through India, talking to people and delivering lectures. It is also possible that he might have studied some books of elocution. His skilful use of rhetorical devices suggests that he was conversant with the guiding principles of rhetoric and *arse predicandi*.

Again, excessive praise and spiritual training that he got from his Guru Ramakrishna further emboldened him. Ramakrishna acclaimed, "if Keshub is possessed of one sign of greatness which has made him famous, Naren has eighteen such signs." His high opinion about Naren was a continuous source of strength and inspiration to him. And he always tried to come upto the expectation of his Guru. A sense of strong self-confidence helped him overcome all inhibition while speaking before men of greater learning and experience.

Above all. the urgency of his spirit to carry out the message of his Guru, his intimacy with Reality and a burning desire to serve the poor, the destitute millions and ailing humanity burst out in his powerful speech. He was immediately elevated to the state of *Yogi*, or *Rishi*, at par with Shankara. The theory of spiritual transmission and the grace of Guru are held in high esteem in India. Swamiji acknowledges it and says that he was a bit nervous before addressing the Parliament but his guru Ramakrishna helped him accomplish the task. By the grace of Ramakrishna, he could experience *Nirvikalpa Samadhi* that he intensely longed for. At his first experience, Ramakrishna predicted:

> Naren will pass away only of his own will. The moment he realizes who he is, he will refuse to stay a moment longer in the body. The time will come when he will shake the world

> to its foundations through the strength of his intellectual and spiritual powers. I have prayed that the Divine Mother may keep this realization of the Absolute veiled from Naren. There is much work to be done by him. (*Life*, I, 178)

From this statement it appears that Ramakrishna trained Naren so that he could translate his words into action. As he professed: "My *siddhis* will manifest through you."

He was so pained to feel the misery of the people that he wanted a mission that could help the poor materially for he realized full well that the bread, cloth and shelter were the crying needs of the people in India. And it demanded a man of *Rajas* that Vivekananda was. Ramakrishna was wholly *Sattva*, and was always guiding and goading him. He made him realize that the Absolute Vedanta alone could reconcile all philosophies. The Samadhi helped him become a distinct writer whose words became *aptvakya* for he got the first hand knowledge of the subject he dealt with in his lectures and writings. Naren had been given spiritual training for four years before he could receive the spiritual inheritance of his master: "O Naren, today I have given you my all and have become a Fakir." (*Life*, I, 182)

To Vivekananda, he was the Krishna of Arjun. So persistent was Vivekananda's scepticism that his master at the end of his life had to say like Shri Krishna: "He who was Rama, He who was Krishna, He himself is now Ramakrishna in this body:" (*Life*, I, 183) Ramakrishna told him that he was the incarnation of Narayana. With this background, the artist and the spiritual yogi in him flourished and carved out his place in the chain of the propounders of Advaita Vedanta.

If the temple of Dakshineshwar enabled him to verify the veracity of the ancient texts and the oneness of all religions that was practically demonstrated by his master, his journey throughout the country from the Himalayas to Cape Comorin made him one with the miseries, poverty and ignorance of the countrymen. During this journey he conversed with saints and prostitutes, kings and beggars, lived in castles and hovels, and learnt the basic unity in all the apparent diversity. This unity is not superficial or on physical plane. It is much broader than what we commonly understand. It is the identification with the whole of creation—animate and inanimate, man and animal, known and unknown, sensuous and supersensuous, the earth and the whole solar system. He developed the essential unity he saw in the Indian life to the highest pedestal of unity through his superconscious state of mind. Like Lord Buddha, he had a realization under a peepul tree at Kakrighat near Almora. He narrated it to Akhandananda and quoted his Eastern and Western Disciples: "Here under this Peepul tree one of the greatest problems of my life has been solved. I have found the oneness of the macrocosm with the microcosm. In this microcosm of the body everything that is there exists. I have seen the whole universe within an atom." (*Life*, I, 250) The realization seems to be reflected in his lecture, "The Cosmos: The Macrocosm and the Microcosm."

The life of *Parivarajak* was the greatest school for him where he got training and first-hand knowledge in many fields; and its influence, one can trace in each and every page of his *Complete Works*. His travel of historical places in India and some in the West made him a true historian. He became conversant with all the philosophical and literary trends and religious sects and movements in and outside India. One can imagine what a wonderful learner he was that he went to Goa to imbibe the Christian theology from original Latin documents that were available only there; and his teacher there was J.P. Alvares. While travelling in the western India he studied French language and French music. He restudied Panini's *Astadhyayi* and Patanjali's *Mahabhashya* from Pandit Narayandas. His disciples quote from an anonymous writer: "During his travels, by turns he realized the essence of Buddhism and Jainism, the spirit of Ramananda and Dayananda. He had become a profound student of Tulsidas and Nischaldas. He had learned all about the saints of Maharashtra and the Alwars and Nayanars of Southern India." (*Life*, I: 392) The pilgrimage helped him overcome his prejudices and fanaticism, broaden his heart, and he learned India's unity in diversity.

One of the greatest influences on his art and mind came from his intensive study of English literature, Western Philosophy, World History, Psychology and occidental books. We do not have any precise account of the influences in the course of his reading, though his disciples have made an attempt in the chapter "The Man in the Making." The deepest influence of his reading was the "Spencerian mode of reasoning in his discussion of the doctrines of the Upanishads and the Vedanta." About the Vedantic conclusion that the inside and the outside of the universe 'are one and the same,' he finds Herbert Spencer and some other modern philosophers endorsing it. One, however, must not be deluded that he owed his concept of Advaita Vedanta to Spencer or J.S. Mill. He interpreted the religion and its classical books like the Vedas, the Upanishads scientifically. He developed his language, style of writing and scholarship by reading foreign classics. The former Vivekananda, a college student, was more prone to these influences. But when he realized Truth in *Nirvikalp Samadhi* and found an answer to all problems in the Advaita Vedanta, he transcended the reason and books. His disciples write:

> He studied the systems of the German philosophers, particularly those of Kant and Schopenhauer. He studied also John Stuart Mill and Auguste Comte, and delved into Aristotelian analysis and speculations. For a time he found satisfaction in the Positivist philosophy of Comte which embraces a wide ethical outlook. (*Life*, I, 102-3)

But he did not accept anything unless it stood true to reason. Like Scott and Hazlitt, he was all for objectivity in the study of a subject. He studied the holy *Koran* and accepted only the truth in it and rejected the superstitious element in it. He went through the *Bible* and *Imitation of Christ* and discovered the wonder that Jesus was and that the Christians failed to understand him and consequently made it 'a shop-keeping religion.' We see him extracting moral meaning from both *The Old* and *The New Testament* of the Hebrews and the *Bhagavad-Gita* while speaking on "Soul, God and Religion." The topic "What is Religion?" bears the reinforcing influence of St. Paul. Vivekananda's speeches and articles like "Vedic Religious Ideals" and "Reincarnation" bear the influence of his wide reading of all religions, ancient civilizations and Indian and Greek mythologies. He was no less influenced by Max Mueller and called him the reincarnation of an Indian sage. His socialism was influenced by Karl Marx and his literature has the Marxian impact to a certain extent.

In his language and style, he came in varying degrees and at various points under the influence of Herbert Spencer, J.S. Mill, Carlyle, Newman, Arnold, Jules Verne and Bacon. But his art of composition and rhetoric was developed and shaped by his personal contact with his college professors. He was a conversationalist like Surendranath Banerjee and a scholar like Professor William Hastie. If his boyish theism owed to his parents, his adolescent scepticism and analytical reasoning owed much to satirical science in general and J.S. Mill's *Three Essays on Religion*, Hume, Spencer and Bacon's inductive method in particular. And the result was a violent Victorian conflict between reason and Universal Reason, science and religion and an impatient thirst to know the Truth that engulfed his mind and soul. His bohemian spirit hankered after solution. He tried diverse teachers, creeds and cults but in vain. He got some solace from Shelley as Dr. Brajendranath Seal, his friend, writes, and his Disciples quote:

> I gave him a course of readings in Shelley. Shelley's hymn to the spirit of intellectual beauty, his pantheism of impersonal love and his vision of a glorified millennial humanity moved him as the arguments of the philosophers had failed to move him. (*Life*, I: 108)

His intensive study of English writers—philosophers, poets, novelists and historians—enable him to evolve a world view that would have remained a far cry in the absence of intensive study. How could he have shown the uniformity in the basic tenets of all religions? If Ramakrishna or Christ could convince their disciples by mystic power or by the efflorescence of Bhakti, Swamiji could do it by the power of wit, intelligence and wisdom. It doesn't mean that his heart did not ache for the delicate love—*bhakti*. But he had to check it with his *Jnana* for he had to accomplish the task assigned to him by his master. A pure *bhaktin* is all *Sattva*, but to bring about the renaissance and the revolution, one requires both *Rajas* and *Sattva*. We may well recall that on this point, Swamiji was misunderstood by his brother disciples and was accused of ignoring Ramakrishna's teachings. Swami Yogananda accused him of propagating his own ideas of "philanthropic activities, organizations, homes of service for the public good, and patriotic work" that he learnt from his western education and his travel abroad. His colleagues believed that Ramakrishna had emphasized *bhakti* alone for the spiritual quest. Swamiji replied:

> When one attains *bhakti*, one's heart and nerves become so soft and delicate that they (sic) cannot bear even the touch of a flower! . . . I cannot think or talk of Shri Ramakrishna long without being overwhelmed. I am trying to bind and bind myself with the iron chain of Jnana, for still my work to my motherland is unfinished. (*Life*, II: 253)

Swamiji was so much overwhelmed that he was about to enter into trance when Swami Yogananda and others changed the conversation and diverted his mind. It was this incident that is supposed to have brought about a crisis in his inner self. They felt that his innermost soul had been awakened and words of his master rang in their ears that the day Narendra knew who he was, he would cease to live in this body. This incident silenced his critics and established the fact that it was Ramakrishna who worked through him.

His approach of teaching and working was genuinely shaped and modelled by his avid reading. Frequent references and allusions drawn from varied sources show his scholarship and the avidity of his readership. He develops a clear concept of history, science, archaeology, philosophy besides various religions. And this enabled him to make a comparative study of religions and to judge his own religion in the light of others. This process of study makes one see the plus and minus points of one's subject clearly and do the required amendments in one's own portfolio. So did the Swami and the result was the renaissance of Upanishadic religion or the birth of 'Neo-Hinduism.'

The sight of Somnath's ruined temple and of many such places gave him an insight into the national life current as he himself says in his lecture "The Future of India":

> Some of these old temples of southern India and those like Somnath of Gujarat will teach you volumes of wisdom, will

> give you a keener insight into the history of the race than any amount of books. Mark how these temples bear the marks of a hundred attacks and a hundred regenerations, continually destroyed and continually springing up out of the ruins, rejuvenated and strong as ever. (*Works*, 3: 289)

Again his indepth study of English provided him with a thesaurus of Saxon words and words of Latin origin that he used with ease and subtlety. He not only grasped the subtlety of English language but also became conversant with various trends in English literature. Through this, he came in contact with the Oxford movement, as a matter of fact, it was aimed at the church that had sunk deep into stagnation. Swamiji had also directed his cannon towards priesthood. Exponents of movement like Keble, Newman and others wanted to replace the old by the new. But Swamiji tried to do away with the priesthood.

Swamiji writes in his "Memories of European Travel": "Monsieur Jules Bois is a famous writer; he is particularly an adept in the discovery of historical truths in the different religions and superstitions. He has written a famous book putting into historical form the devil-worship, sorcery, necromancy, incantation and such other rites that were in vogue in Mediaeval Europe." (*Works*, 7: 375)

The historical form of the philosophic or religious book of Jules Bois that he is talking about can also be found in some of his works. Living in contact with novelists, poets and writers, he might have learnt something new of the craft of writing. His knowledge of Greek owes something to Professor J.H. Wright.

Through his prodigious readings he discovered that the Vedantic ideas had "crept into the great French poets, such as Victor Hugo, Lamertine and others, and the great German poets such as Goethe, Schiller, and the rest. The influence of Vedanta on European poetry and philosophy is very great. Every good poet is a Vedantin, I find; and whoever writes some philosophical treatise has to draw upon Vedanta in some shape or other." (*Works*, 7: 375)

His view of revolution and his iconoclastic ideas are brought home through a profound reflection on the political revolutions—French Revolution, revolution in America for independence and

Opium Wars. His new idea of revolution was the result of his understanding of the political revolutions in European history and the Renaissance in India brought about by Bhakti Movement and Sufism. He discarded violence in revolution for he had been aware of the tragedy of French Revolution. In his speech on "The East and the West" he says: "The whole French nation became mad in the name of liberty and equality. . . . With the edge of the sword and at the point of bayonet he (Napoleon) thrust 'Liberty, Equality and Fraternity' into the very bone and marrow of Europe." (*Works*, 8: 33) Such views have been enshrined in him by his study of history. His authenticity and firmness of ideologies are born of his habit of reading thoroughly the original texts. In him we find the spirit of Krishna, Buddha, Christ, Mohammad and Luther cherished. We know from his writings how he loved and adorned the love of Krishna for Gopis, the intellect of Shankara, the heart of Buddha, the service of Christ to the destitute, the body of Mohammad and Islam's social equality and the rebellious spirit of Luther. His reform movement bears the influence of Luther's protestant movement. He, too, was in a sense protestant. But his protestantism was all positive and constructive and less iconoclastic. His iconoclasm is confined to private discourses and letters and he rarely makes it public.

Buddha was another source of enlightenment for him in whom he finds infinite calm and tranquillity, saintly understatement and negation of everything including the Vedas and other scriptures except the universal soul. In him he finds the acme of Advaita Vedanta and a saviour of mankind. One can see his love and veneration for the *Light of Asia*, a poem on the life of Buddha by Edwin Arnold, and for *Lalita Vistara* in several references to them. Buddha's idea of self sacrifice, his renunciation and his concept of misery that man is at fault for his suffering impressed him. As he quotes from the *Light of Asia*.

> Ye suffer from yourselves. None else compels
> None other holds you that ye live and die,
> And whirl upon the wheel, and hug and kiss
> Its spokes of agony,
> Its tire of tears, its nave of nothingness. (*Works*, I: 407)

He finds the same idea of destiny recurring again and again in the tragedies of Shakespeare in which Macbeth, King Lear, Hamlet and Othello suffer severe misfortune out of their own faults in character.

Light of Asia, *Imitation of Christ* and many such books that he studied thoroughly not only illumined him but also provided him images and symbols. One can notice for example the image of 'wheel' and 'spokes' from the above-quoted stanza employed by Swamiji in his writings.

Again, the words of *Dhammapada* greatly inspired and enthused him in the days of wandering:

> Go forward without a path!.
> Fearing nothing, caring for nothing
> Wander alone, like the rhinoceros!
> Even as the lion, not trembling at noises,
> Even as the wind, not caught in the net. (*Life*, I, 264)

The West with its splendour of materialism, technological and industrial advancement, freedom of women left a lasting impression on his mind and made him advocate the exchange of these with the spiritual property of the East. Though the material splendour soon lost its glamour in his eyes, the idea of material advancement without making any compromise with the spiritual heritage remained ever with him. Swamiji loved Americans for their friendliness of heart and the English for their discipline and forthrightness and work culture.

The Renaissance spirit in Vivekananda bears the impact of religious reform movements launched in various parts of India by Kabir, Chaitanya, Dadu, Ramanujan and Shankaracharya and the Renaissance movement of England in the Elizabethan age. We can see how his Advaita echoes Kabir and rectifies Kabir's limitation by imbibing the love of Chaitanya and the Dualism of Ramakrishna. Kabir outrightly rejects all rituals, temples, etc. Swamiji calls them secondary and recognizes that the virtue lies in them and their importance for the lower rung of the people but calls for a movement from Dualism to Advaitism.

Vivekananda's studies of the Renaissance literature of England brought him close to its ideas. The affinities between the Renaissance literature and the literature of Vivekananda show how much he was influenced by the Renaissance literature. Renaissance literally means 'rebirth' or revival of studies in Greek literature and philosophy. It was a return to man-centred, this-world-centred learning of classical antiquity and associates in itself the scientific spirit to discover the world and man.

In Vivekananda's case, it is his persistent concern for 'man-making religion,' for the human needs—education, food, clothes, shelter—for the development of individuals, for the revival of studies of Sanskrit language and literature that bears the impact of Renaissance. He put man in the centre of his philosophy and explored the divinity within. His individualism and humanism are essentially spiritual but he knows well that there can be no progress in spirituality without physical, material and intellectual strength as he said, "I do not want that God who cannot give food to the hungry millions." But he eschewed the Renaissance in his preponderance of spiritualism; religion and the other-worldliness over materialism. He reached out a synthesis of the two. There is, however, an essential difference between the two. The Renaissance's humanism, individualism, hedonism and such ideals are on material plane but Swamiji talks on a spiritual plane that reconciles material needs as well.

Vivekananda was more a Romanticist than a Classicist, though his ardent love for his Guru, his classical learning and his Spencerian reasoning can be termed as classical elements in him. But he was inspired by the Romantic spirit of liberty, liberalism and 'imaginative flight of faith.' Like a Romanticist, he discarded the trends set by 'Derozio men' in literature. Unlike them, he gave unrestrained expression to India's spiritual glory and took a positive and sympathetic approach to India. He advocated the use of colloquial, everyday language instead of a specialized poetic diction. His language, like a Romantic poet, is simple but expressive. His poetry has something of Romantic poetry particularly the pantheism of Shelley, Wordsworth's 'spontaneous overflow of powerful feelings,' Keatsian love for the Hellenic world, mysticism and visionary spirit of William Blake, and the 'imaginative flight' of the Romantic poets in general. He echoes Blake not only in mysticism and visionary spirit but also in the formlessness of poetry. Unlike the Romantics his zeal for reformation is constructive and not destructive. Similarly on many accounts he departs from the Romantic trends and at times seems to echo the Metaphysicals in his scholarship, in learning, in devotional songs and metaphysical study. We may well recall how modern poets like W.B. Yeats and T.S. Eliot were deeply influenced by it, and the 19th century witnessed the revival of Metaphysical poetry. Vivekananda, like Yeats, made a place for himself in the Metaphysical tradition because of a passionate lifelong desire to weld the world together. Like Donne, he was an intellectual who enjoyed engaging in philosophical arguments and made his learning and logical reasoning an integral part of his writings, at times of his poetry.

One is astonished to see how divergent trends—the learning of East and West, Oriental and Occidental, Classical, Metaphysical and Romantic elements—merge together in Vivekananda to evolve a savant, the prophet of the century with a multifaceted personality.

Swami Vivekananda: The Orator

Swami Vivekananda was *Vir bonus dicendi peritus* (a virtuous man skilled in speaking), to use Cato's definition of an orator. His literature constitutes for the most part a recorded collection of his orations, that he delivered throughout his whirlwind tour of the West for the last nine years of his life. It is a regrettable fact that many of his speeches could not be recorded. From literary point of view he was an orator first and then a writer. The power of his oratory was well acknowledged by the American and the English press. The way he taught the West the whole philosophy of Advaita Vedanta in a foreign language with all force and vitality of a simple but artistic language goes a long way to establish him as a master of *Arse Predicandi*. He was the first preacher of Advaita Vedanta preaching in the West in English language, and he established the spiritual superiority of India over the West.

His speeches and poems are Homeric in the sense that he spoke with a divine inspiration as Homer did. He, however, does not begin his works, except in some poems, with an invocation to muse as Homer did in his epic. Yet time and again, he admits the divine force behind him. Even Plato affirms in his *Dialogues* the divine inspiration of the poet. The same is applicable to the orator. '*Natura ingenium*' is the prerequisite for an orator as insisted on by Cicero throughout his *De Oratore* and *Orator*. It is an inborn quality that cannot be taught; however training and practice (*exercitaio*) and study (*studium*) manifest this quality. Erasmus once said about Bernard that he was a preacher by nature rather than by art. The same can be said about Swamiji.

In *Encyclopaedia America*, oratory is divided into four types:

(1) Forensic (2) Deliberative (3) Occasional (4) Didactic or Philosophical. (1969, 20: 785)

Occasional oratory is a broad class that covers both epideictic and panegyric oratory. B.N. Mittra in his article "Vivekananda: An Orator" writes: "All famous orators from the ancient Greek Orator Pericles to modern orators like Sir Winston Churchill were more or less either political or philosophical orators, but Swamiji's oratory was a combination of all types of oratory." (*Prabudha Bharata*) Though elements of all these forms of oratory can be traced in his speeches but he can be called by and large a philosophical orator. Major Mittra has tried to classify his speeches under the above mentioned heads. He regards his speeches at the Parliament and some other speeches in which he defended Hinduism as forensic oratory, his speeches on the opening and closing day of the Parliament of Religions as occasional, his lectures on "Women in India," "The Great Teachers of the World," "On Lord Buddha," "Christ, My Master" as panegyric and others as philosophical.

But do we not find the element of forensic oratory in his lecture "My Plan of Campaign" when he pleads his own case before the court of the people? Or do we not find the traces of occasional oratory in his 'Paper on Hinduism' when he extols Americans? The evidence of panegyric oratory can be easily noticed throughout his lectures from 'Colombo to Almora' that Major Mittra calls deliberative oratory. It does not mean that they are not so but a generic classification seems far-fetched. Above all, a Vedantic flame burns throughout his speeches. Even when he speaks on "My Master," he paints his sketch in the background of Hindu religion, culture and tradition. Therefore we may well appreciate his oratory without making a hard and fast classification of it, in the light of the guiding principles laid down by classical masters. It has not yet been discovered whether he read Cicero and Quintilian or not. But he has studied Aristotle and Plato, and both have rhetorical treatise *Rhetoric* and *Phaderus* respectively to their credit. We come to know from his travelogue "Memoirs of European Travel" that he was well conversant with the Greek and Roman art and history in general. In it he writes in brief about Asiatic and Attic style. Whether he studied them or not, he honoured some of their guiding principles. Ancient rhetoric constitutes of five parts: Invention, Disposition, Elocution, Memory and Delivery. In one form or another these are present in his Oratory. He was ingenious in inventing arguments, skilled in arranging his ideas in order leading them to a logical conclusion and his memory was unique as he spoke without any note or preparation. For the delivery and elocution he was widely praised. *Appeal Avalanche* reports (Jan. 17, 1894):

> The speaker differs in one respect in particular from some American orators. He advances his ideas with as much deliberation as a professor of mathematics (sic) demonstrates an example in algebra to his students. Kananda (sic) speaks with perfect faith in his own powers and ability to hold successfully his position against all argument. He advances no ideas, nor makes assertions that he does not follow up to a logical conclusion. (*Works*, 7: 419-20)

Before we take up his speeches and judge them in the light of the guiding principles laid down by classical masters, we must take a brief look at what makes Vivekananda sway the intelligentsia of America and the Europe. He was one of the youngest delegates in the Parliament of Religions attended by eminent scholars of the world much older and experienced than he was. Yet he accomplished the first task of a good orator assigned by Cicero "not only to make the audience understand but render them impossible not to understand" in the very first attempt. One may ask what makes this alien do so in a foreign land? It is the gesture and posture of the preacher that creates the first impression on the audience. To describe his gesture at the time when he, for the first time, arose to address the Parliament, it is better to quote *St. Louis Observer* of September 21, 1893.

> With his black, curly locks thrown back from his broad brow, his keen, clear eye fixed upon the audience, his long brown finger emphasizing the utterances of his vibrant voice, he looked the very image of a propagandist, and one trembled to know that such a figure stood at the head of the movement to consolidate all the disciples of Buddha and to spread 'the light of Asia.' (Burke, 81)

His very gesture sent a message of universal brotherhood. As for his posture and dress, he was young and dangerously handsome with his athletic physique. His unusual robe arose a curious interest in the audience. Their eyes kept staring at him. *Chicago Advocate* describes him, "In certain respects the most fascinating personality was the Brahmin monk, Swami Vivekananda with his flowing orange robe, saffron turban, smooth-shaven, shapely, handsome face, large, dark subtle penetrating eye." (Burke, 87)

The audience responded to his first address "Sisters and Brothers of America" with aplomb that lasted for a few minutes and it shows as if they were mentally prepared for it. It recaptures the essence of William Thackeray's address: "O brothers . . . O brothers! Speaking the same dear mother tongue—O comrades! enemies no more . . . and call a truce to battle." (Gilkes and Ellingworth) But Thackeray is more dramatic than he is. But what did prepare them for such reception? Obviously, it was his regal bearing, divinely radiating gesture, hypnotic posture, dress and Christ-like simplicity of manner and above all the blessing of Shri Ramakrishna that prepared the ground for stirring people's emotion to its depth. Above all it is the personality of the man that leaves the deepest and longest impression on our mind. Swamiji himself says: "the personality of man is two thirds, and his intellect, his words are but one third. It is the real man, the personality of the man that runs through us." He stands identical with Aristotle who maintains that orator in the course of oration establishes an ethos—a personal character which itself functions as a means of persuasion.

As for his words, they are emotionally charged, well picked up and 'sensational' like those of Donne. His addresses in the Parliament except his 'Paper on Hinduism' are not subtle and perhaps not his best. These speeches are to some extent reminiscent of the Edwardian and Marian preachers who did not argue deeply but aimed at hitting the popular fancy. But he does not fall into artifice as they did. His appeal, here, primarily lies to emotion and sentiment that is regarded by Cicero as 'the highest power of an orator.' These speeches can be called panegyric oratory. To quote a few emotive passages from his addresses at the Parliament:

> It fills my heart with joy unspeakable to rise in response to the warm and cordial welcome which you have given us. I

> thank you in the name of the most ancient order of monks in the world; I thank you in the name of the mother of religions; and I thank you in the name of millions and millions of Hindu people of all classes and sects. (*Works*, I: 3)

The magnificence of the address lies in two things—first the negative capability of the speaker and second the emotive language. By using 'us' instead of 'me' he turns the welcome given to him to all. Again, he thanks but in the name of somebody else. The emphasis is on 'millions and millions of Hindus.' The message implied in it is that the Hindu religion is 'stretching its arms' to embrace all. Whatever applause given to him, being an emulator of the *Gita*, he cannot attach himself to it. It was not he but 'the religious consciousness of India that spoke through him.' Secondly, the structural parallelism strengthened by the repetition of the principal clause "I thank you" creates a sonorous rhythmic effect on the mind of the audience.

He continues to whip up emotion to erase and ease out the feelings of hatred and discrimination for the Hindu from the mind of the American people:

> Allow me to call you, brethren, by that sweet name—heirs of immortal bliss—yea, the Hindu refuses to call you sinners. Ye are the children of God, the sharers of immortal bliss . . Ye divinities on earth—sinners! It is a sin to call a man so . . . Come up O lions, and shake off the delusion that you are sheep; you are souls immortal, spirits free, blest and eternal. (*Works*, I: 11)

Swamiji's emphatic rap in the speech "Ye divinities on earth—sinners" shook the fundamental notion of the Christian that men are in a state of original sin after the fall. The speaker displays his mastery of rhetorical style by giving pauses, by repeating the image of 'immortal bliss' frequently and using other images like 'ye divinities,' 'soul,' 'lion,' 'spirit' to reinforce the same idea and by the artistic arrangement of words, fully charged with evocative spirit, by invocations and exclamations. He succeeded in infusing into the souls of his hearers a plea of sovereign and sublime virtue and in relieving the friction by his homeopathic treatment with words of praise. All this makes it a classical piece of Oratory. Some more examples of emotional appeal can be cited: "May he who is the Brahman of the Hindus, the Ahur-Mazada of the Zoroastrians, the Buddha of the Buddhists, the Jehovah of the Jews, the Father in Heaven of the Christians, give strength to you to carry out your noble idea!" (*Works*, I: 19-20) Or again, "Hail, Columbia, Motherland of liberty!"

All such appeasing, passionate speeches are astutely aimed at winning the favour of the audience, preparing the favourable ground for the exposition of the more complex ideas of universal religion and for getting financial support for India. Like an ambassador, he was pleading the case of India: "I came here to seek aid for my impoverished people."

His speeches at the Parliament begin and end in a formulaic pattern. His beginning gives a hint of what he is going to plead and his end culminates the polemic ideas carried throughout the middle into an emotional and reasoned appeal and hope. Each ends with a note of hope except the one he spoke on 20th September, 1893 on "Religion Is Not The Crying Need of India," "I fully realized how difficult it was to get help for heathens from Christians in a Christian land." (*Works*, I: 20)

As for the formulaic pattern, take for example his second speech "Why We Disagree." Taking the question from his earlier speaker that was left unanswered, he answers the question by telling a story: "I will tell a little story" and then the story follows and the speech ends with a note of hope, "hope that, in the future, the Lord will help you to accomplish your purpose."

Again, when he reads his "Paper on Hinduism," he starts with the three ancient religions "Hinduism, Zoroastrianism and Judaism." The latter two virtually eclipsed from the modern world and what remained was Hinduism that he discussed. Throughout the pages he expounds the polemic ideas of the catholicity and universality of the Hindu religion and authenticated it by alluding to and quoting from scriptures, enlivens it by parables, anecdotes and reminiscences. His words come out from the depth of truth verified by his own experiences and observations. Sister Nivedita rightly says about this paper: "It may be said that when he began to speak, it was 'the religious ideas of the Hindus' but when he ended, Hinduism had been created." (Introduction, *Works*) Swamiji draws parallels between the beliefs of Hinduism and the basic theories of modern science. The speech culminates in an appeal to America "to march at the vanguard of civilization with the flag of harmony."

The same emphasis on harmony can be heard in his final address: "upon the banner of every religion will soon be written, in spite of resistance: 'Help and not Fight,' 'Assimilation and not Destruction,' 'Harmony and Peace and not Dissension.'" (*Works*, 224) These are the prophetic words uttered by the 'prophet of a New Dispensation.' At the Parliament, he also denounces the "workshop" religion of the Christian missionaries and their pseudo-charity works in India so mildly and cleverly that his denunciation is endorsed in the Parliament. He seems to be a Martin Luther in his denunciation of the religion of Pope. Martin Luther while defending himself before Charles V delivered a virulent oratorical speech in periodic sentences: "The sufferings and complaints of all mankind are my witnesses, that, through the laws of the Pope and the doctrines of men, the conscience of the faithful have been ensnared, tortured, and torn in pieces." (Gilkes and Ellingworth, 27) The speech seems to be uttered in a single breath extempore. Compared to it Swamiji's language is milder and sentences are short and simple. The speech contains the same intensity of feeling and impetuosity:

> It matters not as long as India is true to herself and to her religion. But a blow has been struck at her heart by this awful godless West when she sends hypocrisy and atheism into her midst. Instead of sending bushels of abuses, carloads of vituperation and shiploads of condemnations, let an endless stream of love go forth. (*Works*, 2: 517)

About his speeches at the Parliament, it may be said that he employed a simple style for stirring the audiences' mind and reaching the people. He was very much conscious of the theory of decorum. Nowhere else had he delivered such a formal and enchanting address. Nowhere else had he been so much conscious of the mind of the audience. Elsewhere, in most cases, he spoke what he had to say—be it appeasing or inciting to hearers. He took least care of it. His oration, here, is an example of forensic oratory in the sense that he was pleading before a jury of all sects the case of Hinduism and of India in a logical, argumentative way rendering facts of its universality and the malady of Christian missionary's work in India; and he won the case by getting his criticism endorsed by the Parliament. If the impression of the audience is any test for successful oratory, he proved himself beyond doubt a successful orator. The Americans, especially women, flocked round him. Huge crowds cheered him wherever he went and whenever he spoke. From his *Life* we come to know that he was a vast crowd puller and was made to speak at the end of the day lest the audience should leave the venue. Miss Monarac writes in her autobiography *A Poet's Life* that it was "a rare and perfect moment of supreme emotion. It was human eloquence at its highest pitch." John Henry Wright writes: "he is one of the best educated men in the world." Hundreds of newspaper reporters flocked around him and declared him the hero of the Parliament. His command over English language was instantly recognized. *Chicago Advocate* that was critical of him admitted: "His knowledge of English is as though it were his mother tongue." *Boston Evening Transcript*, Sept. 23 writes that "He speaks excellent English." At the Parliament, he spoke in the language of the people devoid of all technicalities and obscurity. He read the English translation of Sanskrit Verse from the scriptures. Though he had a good knowledge of Latin and French, he did not use Latin and French words and expressions. About his language, Marie Louise Burke writes: "he deliberately couched his message in language as simple and untechnical as possible, for his intention was to reach the people with words and ideas meaningful to all. He was a world Teacher not a pedant. But when the occasion called for a scholarly presentation of Hinduism, as it did at the scientific section, where sharp-minded philosophers, theologians and scholars came to learn and perhaps to challenge, he very likely gave as much rein to his vast learning as was necessary." (94) If oratory is considered as the science of persuasion as Isocrates called it, the orator can persuade by reason or by emotion. Swamiji persuaded by both; and so much ovation and acclamation he got that it made him weep.

He was conscious of the fact that to move the audience is only a preliminary task of a preacher, the task ahead is to teach the Advaita Vedanta to the West. As for the third principle—to delight, it should be noted that he hardly spoke anything for this end. Whenever delight came, it came through his exemplums, fables, parables, reminiscences, anecdotes and ironical quips in his speech. But the purpose of all these is to teach and not to delight. For instance, he gave a short address at the parliament on "Why We Disagree" through an exemplum of the frog in the well. Each frog thinks that this little well is the whole world. So like those frogs everyone thinks that his religion is the only truth. As a matter of fact exemplums, fables and parables are common in the text of a sermon. Exemplum was a popular device in the Middle ages when extensive collections of it were published for use by preachers. It can also be found in Chaucer's *The Pardoner's Tale* in which the pardoner, preaching on the thesis "Greed is the root of all evil," uses the exemplum of three revellers who set out to find Death but find a treasure and kill one another in the attempt to get it.

Like exemplum, parable too, has always been the favourite device of a preacher. Buddha, Christ, Ramakrishna taught more through parables and fables. Emma Calve writes about Vivekananda in her autobiography: "He often spoke in parables, answering our questions or making his points clear by means of poetic analogy," Then she quotes his parable that he told her to make her understand the theory of incarnation:

> One day a drop of water fell into the vast ocean, when it found itself there, it began to weep and complain just as you are doing. The great ocean laughed at the drop of water. "Why do you weep?" it asked: "I do not understand. When you join all your brothers and sisters. . . . If you wish to leave me, you have only to rise up on a sunbeam into the clouds. From there you can descend again little drop of water, a blessing and a benediction to the thirsty earth. (*Life*, I: 450-51)

And again he tells, "The story of the man who wanted a ghost to work for him but who, when he had the ghost, could not keep him employed, until he gave him a curly dog's tail to straighten."

(*Works*, 4: 206) By this story he draws a parallel between our case and the case in the story with the ghost. This shows how practical he is. He does not live in a fool's paradise; rather he knows the reality that he or for that matter anybody else however great cannot make the world free from all evils.

He also narrates the Christian story "of the young lady and the clergyman," who were both looking at the moon through the telescope and seeing the moon spots the clergyman said, "I am sure they are the spires of some churches." "Nonsense," said the young lady, "I am sure they are the young lovers kissing each other." (*Works*, 4: 207) But he does not delve deep into them. Since the audiences were familiar with them, simple reference to the story for instance the story of deluge, of Medona, at times meets his purpose.

He uses a fable, in his lecture "Soul, God and Religion," of a cub of lion that was 'brought up in the flock, who ate grass and bleated like a sheep.' It remained a sheep until a lion came and showed it its image in the water. So we are like that lion unknown of our reality, bleating as a man while we are divine, god. The concept that man is god, immortal while men are dying each day is so abstruse particularly for the Western mind that it demands a parable or fable to make it comprehensible.

Again while speaking on the topic "What is Religion?" he simplifies the philosophy of Advaita and makes it digestible to the audience by using another fable of two birds sitting on a tree, 'one on the top, another below.' The bird below was eating one moment a sweet fruit, another a bitter one. He looked up and saw the other bird 'calm and majestic.' 'He came near the other bird' and was enveloped in the rays of light and was changed into the higher bird. 'And he found that there had been but one bird all the time on the tree.' 'The lower bird was but the reflection of the one above.' The story shows how we are one with the Lord. This material world is but Maya. The need is to rise above the plane of Maya and to identify ourselves with the reality. But to know the reality we need one who has realized the divinity.

Though some more examples of fables and parables can be found in his formal speeches, but he did not speak in parables as much as Christ and Ramakrishna did. He, however, used these devices wherever he found it necessary to simplify the abstruse concept of Advaita philosophy. They are functional and not decorative. We have more analogy and less parables and fables. In fact no single device of *Arse predicandi* is enough for him to imprint his theories on the mind of the audience. His favourite rhetorical devices are: repetition of words, ideas and quotations, allusions, and references to scriptures, questions followed by answers and at times rhetorical questions, polemic development of ideas, illustrations, simple and hypothetical sentence structures and images and figures of speech. These are frequently used devices. Besides these, we cannot overlook the use of Sanskrit words, pauses, digressions and other linguistic and stylistic devices. In the sincerity of feeling and intensity of clerical eloquence, he is no less than Taylor, Wesley and Newman. But he comes closer to Wesley than to Taylor: "To-day, give up thyself, thy body, thy soul and spirit to God through Christ Jesus,' desiring nothing but that God may be glorified in all thou art, all thou doest all thou sufferst; seeking nothing but to know God." (Giles and Ellingworth, 31-32) The same perceptual exhortion can be noticed in Swamiji's lecture "What Is Religion?": "Get rid, in the first place of all these limited ideas and see God in every person—working through all hands, walking through all feet, and eating through every mouth." (*Works*, 341) The former seems more intense, impatient and exhorting, but the latter's concept is more sublime and the tone saintly. The effect of 'God in every person' is intensified by the repetition of gerund form 'working through,' 'walking through' and 'eating through.' It reflects almost an 'Upanisadic intensity.'

Swamiji belongs to the 'liberal' school of orators and bears the impact of Macaulay on his prose-style in amplitude and richness of phrasing and weight of miscellaneous learning. But there is hardly any artifice and embellishments. That is why he abandons the severity of treatise and speaks or writes not for the specialists as Aristotle or in modern times T.S. Eliot did but for that wider public which Plato had in mind. In this respect Swamiji and T.S. Eliot stand in opposition. The former advocates the spread of culture and religion 'deluge the world with religion' while the latter wants to preserve it by not letting it come to the commoners. Being a preacher, he had to reach the people and hence in art he comes close to Leo Tolstoy who stressed on the aspect of communication in art.

Like Donne, he is more concerned with his material—the delivery of his thoughts. As he says: "What matters it whether you speak correct grammar or with fine rhetoric? What matters it whether your language is ornamental or not? The question is whether or not you have anything to give. . . . If you have, then give. Words but convey the gift: it is but one of the many modes." (*Works*, 4: 123-24)

In some respects Vivekananda is comparable with Donne. Both are preachers and both believe in the immortality of soul. They drive home the subtle scholastic arguments through parables and exemplums as well as by the use of homely idioms and images. But Donne's language is more rich in sensuousness, colour, ornament and in metaphysical images. In language, the two cannot be compared. Swamiji's age was the Romantic and the Victorian one. Even in England, an urge for simplicity in language was the prime feature of the age. Both spoke in the language of their own age. Let us see how and what Donne spoke on soul at the Earl of Bridgewater's house in London in 1627:

> There are so many evidences of the immortality of the soule, even to a naturall man's *reason*, that it required not an article of the Creed, to fix this notion of the Immortality of the soule. But the Resurrection of the Body is discernible by no other light, but that of *Faith*, nor could be fixed by any lesse assurance than an *Article* of the *Creed*. Where be all the splinters of that Bone, which a shot hath shivered and scattered in the Ayre? Where be all the atoms of that flesh, which a *Corrasive* hath breath'd, and exhal'd away from our arms, and other *Limbs*? In what wrinkle, in what furrow, in what bowel of the earth, lay all the grains of the ashes of a body burnt a thousand years since? In what corner, in what ventricle of the sea, lies all the jelly of a body drowned in the *generall flood*? What coherence, what sympathy, what dependence maintains any relation, any correspondence, between that arm that was lost in Europe, and that leg that was lost in Africa or Asia, scores of years between. (Ford, 3: 119)

We may well set against this undoubtedly fine and rhetorical piece of prose a passage from Swamiji on a similar theme:

> The different philosophies seem to agree that this Atman, whatever it be, has neither form nor shape must be omnipresent. Time begins with mind, space also is in the mind. Causation cannot stand without time. Without the idea of succession, there cannot be any idea of causation. Time, space and causation, therefore, are in the mind, and as this *Atman* is beyond the mind and formless; it must be beyond time, beyond space, and beyond causation. Now, if it is beyond time, space and causation, it must be infinite. Then comes the highest speculation in our philosophy. The infinite cannot be two. If the soul be infinite there can be only one soul, and all ideas of various souls . . . are not real. The real Man, therefore, is one and infinite; the omnipresent Spirit. And the apparent man is only a limitation, of that Real Man. (*Works*, 2: 78)

In both passages, it is difficult to cut across the constant jet of thought. But the former is emotional, sensual and more rhetorical, while the latter is logical and intellectual. Donne achieves the fire and motion of oratory through recurrent questionings, repetitions and alliterations. Donne speaks on the familiar subject in a dualistic vein of Christianity. But both, like other orators, depend heavily upon rhetorical questions and repetition to invite emotional responses to shake off the pre-established notions and to imprint new ideas. Swamiji here is introducing a concept new to them. So the need is not of the fire of emotion but of the logical reasoning. Like Donne's, there is no overlay of ideas. But there is a polemic progression of ideas beginning from simple Atman and coming to its acme in the grandest philosophy of the 'Real Man' that human mind has ever thought of. The whole discussion centres round the principal concept that he wants to drive home; and it is the common feature in his lectures. In general, however, he is more akin to Lancelot Andrewes than to Donne in his keenly argued discourses and ordering of ideas. Like a teacher, he puts a question and then answers it and the process goes on in most of his explanatory speeches.

At times, he presents different views on the question before giving the Vedantic conclusion. This can best be found in his lectures on 'Jnana-Yoga' in London—for example in the lecture "The Real Nature of Man" he talks about Nihilistic approach and some other philosophies about *Atman*, draws the point of similarity and of difference among them and shows how Vedantic conclusion is the most reasonable one. Again in the same group of lecture "Maya and the Conception of God"—one of the most allusive lectures—he traces the various shades of the concept of God from *Samhita*, the scriptures of Greeks, Persian, Hebrews, the Christians (The Old Testament), the Charvaka, the Buddhist and finally shows the culmination of these thoughts into the supreme Advaitic concept of 'Upanishadic God.' It is again in this group that we find the most illustrative lectures—particularly his speech on the concept of *Maya* is one of the best examples of illustrative oratory. The absence of a proper word in English for *Maya* necessitated it. The word *Maya* is commonly taken for the word delusion in English but not so by Swamiji. It is, in him, 'a statement of fact of the world.' Just one example will suffice:

> Then there is the tremendous fact of death. . . . Saints die and sinners die. Kings die and beggars die. They are all going to death, and yet this tremendous clinging on to life exists. Somehow, we do not know why, we cling to life; we cannot give it up. And this is Maya. (*Works*, 2: 92-93)

Syntactical parallelism combined with phonological stress and pitch elements achieve a subtle rhythmic effect in the passage. There can be many such examples but it is impossible to isolate purely phonological effects; for they are part of a complex of lexical, syntactical and stress devices interweaving phonology and meaning. For example: "Cities come and go, empires rise and fall, planets break into pieces and crumble into dust to be blown about by the atmospheres of other planets." (*Works*, 2: 93) Besides syntactical parallelism, balanced antithesis and the phonological effect of the alliteration of 'b' explosive sound heightens the effect.

After sowing the seeds of Vedanta in America and England, Vivekananda sailed for his beloved motherland. On way he landed first at Colombo and was accorded a warm welcome by the Hindus (Tamil) of Sri Lanka. Similarly he got an enthusiastic reception wherever he went from Colombo to Almora; he addressed the people at several places in between. His lectures from Colombo to Almora can be grouped into deliberative oratory for he puts forth his further plan of action, his mission as well as the dual role that India has to play—of a teacher and of a student. But his reply to the address in which he extols the individuals, particularly Rajas is a case of occasional oratory. He exhorts the people in the strongest terms that India has to come out to teach spirituality to the West and at the same time is ready to learn science and technology. To establish a relation of equality, India has to give her share in the development of civilization or else She will be condemned to remain a beggar.

In many respects this group of oratory differs from his Parliamentary ones or from his addresses in the West after the Parliament but internally the same flame burns. The difference is in subject, language and style. Some changes in the language and style are owing to the reason that these were not taken down in shorthand and only a summary was produced later on by a third person. So the language has missed the Vivekanandian touch although the writer has tried his best to reproduce the speech. However, we are not going to make a semantic study of Vivekananda's language. In these speeches his main concern is to awake the Indian masses from their long stupor. He adorns India's past glory and her superiority in the field of religion over the world in an ornate and elegant style. "There is an eternal fountain of spirituality in our scriptures, and nowhere on earth, except in this land of renunciation, do we find such noble example of practical spirituality." (*Works*, 3: 134)

We hardly find such an emphatic and aggressive assertion of India's superiority in his lectures in the West. Their force lies in the choice of sublime words 'eternal fountain of spirituality' with the alliteration of 't' sound and the opulence of vowels in making them high sounding and in the use of three emphasizers 'nowhere,' 'except' and 'do' in one sentence. The phrase 'eternal fountain of spirituality' also suggests a sense of propriety in the use of diction, for the epithet is from our most holy scripture.

Vivekananda's speeches largely run with this kind of ovation and adulation for Hinduism reminding the countrymen that religion is their backbone as politics and social reform are the backbones of England and America respectively and, at the same time, teaching them his religion of Vedanta that had not received its due consideration from the people. And India had nothing to be praised for but its past religious glory, so says Derozio in his poem "My Native Land." The poet does not hide anything but Swamiji, knowing the fact full well, converts the people's mind from present decadent plight to past pristine glory and calls upon the people to do better than their glorious ancestors did: "Our ancestors did most wonderful works, and we look back upon their work with veneration and pride. But we also are going to do great deeds, and let others look back with blessings and pride upon us as their ancestors." (*Works*, 3: 135)

A sense of conviction, confidence and urgency is conveyed by the use of continuous tense 'going to do.' In the first lecture from which we have cited above two examples, he deals with 'Vedantism.' He had also spoken on this subject in America but there he was more analytic and illustrative. Here the lecture was less analytic and more introductory in nature. He spoke straightforwardly. Another difference is in the use of technical Sanskrit words and mantras. There was no more philosophizing and no more plethora of argument. Though he showed his preference for Advaitism but he often talked in dualistic terms considering the people's temperament. For in India, as he himself admits, "We are more Puranic or Tantric than Vedantic." This shows that he was always conscious of the sense of decorum that a good orator ought to have according to Cicero and Quintilian. Another difference is that in the West he expounded the common bases in all religions while in India he showed the common grounds in all sects of a religion. All sects in Hindu religion—be it a dualist, qualified dualist, monist, Shavist, Vaishnavite or any other—have the Vedas as their authority. They all believe in God, Soul, Nature, in the word *Om*, reincarnation; and their moral ethics are by and large the same. Vivekananda does not give much weight to the difference in details though he points out the difference. He says: "If certain forms and formularies help you to realize the Divine, God speed you; have, by all means, whatever forms, and whatever temples, and whatever ceremonies you want to bring you nearer to God. But do not quarrel about them." (*Works*, 3: 132) He reminds them of the theory of *Istha* and welcomes the variation: "Variety is the very soul of life. . . . Your way is very good for you, but not for me. My way is good for me but not for you." (*Works*, 3: 131)

He has no quarrel with any religion in the world but he is against the imposition of one's thought upon another. He minces no words in praising all religions and the concept of personal God. But he does not shrink from showing the superiority of the concept of Impersonal God: "I understand the wonderful flow of love that comes from the idea of a Personal God, . . . What we now want in our country, however, is not so much of weeping, but a little strength. What mine of strength is in this Impersonal God." (*Works*, 3: 130)

In the Parliament of Religions when he was asked to criticize Buddhism he, instead of doing so, adored it and called it the 'fulfilment of Hinduism.' But in India he took opportunity of calling it 'a rebel child of Hinduism.' The idea conveyed is, to some extent, the same but the tone is very different. He uses invectives to expose the degradation that later Buddhism caused to Hinduism. To Christianity he used the invective of 'patchy imitation' of Hinduism. He did not spare even Hinduism and in a mild ironical tone he says in his Address at Manamadura: "There is a danger of our religion getting into the kitchen. We are just 'Don't-touchist' (*Works*, 3: 167) and warns the people that if it continues they will be in "a lunatic asylum" in a century.

Like a satirist he uses mild invectives, sarcasm and irony whenever he talks of the present condition prevailing in India. In the West perhaps he kept his agony reserved for this occasion; and he burst out with his unusual bitterness: "You cannot manufacture one pin, and you dare to criticize the British!" Elsewhere his tone is light: "The West is groaning under the tyranny of the Shylocks, and the East is groaning under the tyranny of the priest; each must keep the other in check." (*Works*, 3: 158) He alludes to Shylock, the Jew in the *Merchant of Venice*, as a symbol of materialists and thinks that each needs something of the other. At another place, he says, "if you go to Varanasi, and sit for five minutes in one of the Ghats there . . . you will see a regular bull-fight going on about these various sects and things." (*Works*, 3: 348) The irony is implied in the image of 'bull-fight.' The animal imagery is deliberately used to scorn this tendency.

Vivekananda speaks in rhetorical irony when he laughs at the so-called reformers: "But in modern times we all want to be called Janakas! They are all Janakas [fathers] of children—unclad, ill-fed, miserable children. The word Janaka can be applied to them in that sense only; they have none of the shining, Godlike thoughts as the old Janaka had. These are our modern Janakas." (*Works*, 3: 343)

In his lecture at Calcutta, he diverts his sarcasm to expose the fallacy of Ramanuja's concept of *Ahara*, "If food alone would purify the sattva, then feed the monkey with milk and rice all its life; would it become a great Yogi?" But this illustration makes an irony of itself and is tantamount to unnecessary exaggeration. For a monkey can by means become a Yogi. And above all, Ramanuja does not say that food alone can make one Yogi. Vivekananda here evades the question whether *Ahara Suddho* means 'food' as Ramanuja took it or 'thought contained in the mind' as Sankar interpreted it.

But his satire, though 'aimed at correction of vices in religion,' never tends to be lampooning. His irony is aimed at irrational practices and not at individuals. He is full of praise for Buddha and Christ but satirizes the degeneration in their religions.

From the rhetorical point of view, his lecture "My Plan of Campaign" delivered at Madras is perhaps the most powerful, moving and personal in subject. It was the first lecture in which he publicly narrated his bitter experiences in America. He came down heavily upon the Theosophists, Brahmo Samaj's leaders and those of Christian missionaries. P.C. Mazumdar, though he does not name him, is the one main target of his virulent attack. He comes out as an aggressive orator unmasking the baseness of these societies and their leaders. To meet the rhetorical need, he hurls a volley of rhetorical questions. Balanced antithesis, periodical sentences, rhetorical repetition of emotive words and phrases, conversational question are some of the common devices he employed to realize the desired effect. He introduced his subjects in these words: "I want . . . to speak a few bold words to you all. There have been certain circumstances growing around me, tending to thwart me, oppose my progress, and crush me out of existence if they could." (*Works*, 3: 339)

The opening note reminds one of Antonio's speech after Caesar's murder in which he creates a suspense by way of letting the people know about Caesar's will. The people become excited to know what was in the will. Similarly, Vivekananda makes people curious to know by hinting at what happened to him in America. He creates the suspense by reserving it for the next day.

Beginning with the Theosophical Society, he takes up one after another and exposes their hypocrisy and meanness. He admits India's indebtedness to Mrs. Annie Besant, but differentiates between having reverence for some one and swallowing everything anyone has to say. He questions all of them in bold terms:

> What harm does it do to the Christian missionary that the Hindus are trying to cleanse their own houses? What injury will it do to the Brahmo Samaj and other reform bodies that the Hindus are trying their best to reform themselves? Why should they stand in opposition? Why should they be the greatest enemies of these movements? Why?—I ask. (1990: 3: 208)

The successive questions culminate into an emphatic 'why?'' It is an effective tool to evoke emotive response from the audience. He also wins the sympathy of the people when he narrates in a personal tone how he 'a poor, unknown, friendless Sannyasin' was denied a letter of introduction from the leader of the Theosophical society. He quotes a brief talk that gives a living effect of that time:

> He asked me, "Will you join my Society?" "No," I replied, "How can I? For I do not believe in most of your doctrines." "Then, I am sorry, I cannot do anything for you." As if not content with this, a Theosophist wrote from India "Let the devil die of cold." (*Works*, 3: 208)

In this kind of expository and revealing oratory, he gets full sympathy even from the reader who has nothing of the living touch of his oration. Take for example this expository passage that evokes sympathy for the hero and anger for the villains.

> They joined the other opposition—the Christian missionaries. There is not one black lie imaginable that these latter did not invent against me. They blackened my character from city to city, poor and friendless though I was in a foreign country. They tried to oust me from every house and to make every man who became my friend my enemy. They tried to starve me out; and I am sorry to say that one of my own countrymen took part against me in this. (*Works*, 3: 20)

The indirect reference is to Brahmo Samaj leader P.C. Mazumdar who was once his friend. We know more about this episode from his *Life*. To counter the misgiving spread by him, he distributed cyclostyled copies of Mazumdar's article in which he had praised Ramakrishna. In this course he answered a few filthy charges levelled against him, particularly the silly charge that he is a Sudra. His racial pride burst out: "In Bengal alone, my blood has furnished them with their greatest philosopher, the greatest poet, the greatest historian, the greatest archaeologist, the greatest religious preacher; my blood has furnished India with the greatest of her modern scientists." (*Works*, 3: 211) The force lies in the recurrent and rhetorical repetition of the emotive adjective 'greatest.' And then he turns to the other side of the charge and declares: "If I am a Pariah, I will be all the more glad, for I am the disciple of a man, who—the Brahmin of Brahmins—wanted to cleanse the house of a pariah." (*Works*, 3: 211) He ends this talk with a hyperbolic sentence that is aimed at the hollowness of his detractors: "One ounce of practice is worth twenty thousand tons of big talk." (*Works*, 3: 212)

He shifts his subject to social reform but speaks in the same vein. Here, he propounds his views on social reform; and is persuasive and argumentative. He calls himself a greater reformer but distinguishes his method by saying that his is constructive one while others are destructive. His offensive stand continues. We may quote one such scornful and satiric remark for the so-called reformer of Madras:

> Boys, moustached babies, who never went out of Madras, standing up and wanting to dictate laws to three hundred millions of people with thousands of traditions at their back. Are you not ashamed? Stand back from such blasphemy and learn first your lessons! Irreverent boys, simply because you can crawl a few lines upon paper and get some fool to publish them . . . you think you are the public opinion of India! Is it so? (*Works*, 3: 219)

It is the honesty and audacious boldness of his speech that is typical of Vivekananda who can speak without minding the response that it can generate. The same audacity can be found in the speeches of Mahatma Gandhi but he lacks the orderly presentation and colour of rhetorical style. K.R. Srinivasa Iyengar writes: "Gandhi lashed right and left much as Jesus chased the money chargers out of the temple." Swamiji did the same more scathingly in a satiric vein. Gandhiji's concept of truth and non-violence bears the influence of Swamiji but he has hardly anything of his oratory. Gandhi speaks in bare colourless language in simple style. We see how the same thing is expressed in two different styles. Gandhiji criticizes Western materialism in these words: "Western nations are today groaning under the heel of the monster God of materialism." Swamiji speaks the same thing in an allusive and precise language: "The West is groaning under the tyranny of Shylock." He hurls to the audience a volley of questions—thirteen questions successively—of which the first one and the last four are rhetorical ones and in them lies the greater force:

> Did India ever stand in want of reformers? Do you read the history of India? Who was Ramunaja? Who was Shankara? Who was Nanak? . . . Who was Dadu? Who were all these great preachers, one following the other, a galaxy of stars of the first magnitude? Did not Ramanuja feel for the lower classes? Did he not try all his life to admit even the pariah to his community? Did he not try to admit even Mohammedans to his own fold? Did not Nanak confer with Hin-

> dus and Mohammedans, and try to bring about a new state of things? They all tried, and their work is still going on. (*Works*, 3: 219)

Interrogation of various kinds has always been a favourite in the armoury of an orator. A rhetorical question is basically a question not expecting an answer or one in which the answer is implied for stylistic effect when the speaker is trying to work up the emotional effect. Vivekananda also uses another type of rhetorical question—a series of questions in quick succession for emphasis. Second, third, fourth, fifth and sixth questions in this passage belong to this group. His rhetorical questions generated the kind of emotional effect Cicero did in these lines:

> Does freedom, that precious things mean nothing? Not the proud privilege of a citizen of Rome? Nor the law of Percius, the laws of Sempronius? Nor the tribune's power, whose loss our people felt so deeply till now at last it has been restored to them? (Gilkies and Ellingwroth, 19)

There is yet another type of rhetorical question that Vivekananda uses—a question put to another person or to himself which expresses surprise or anger and which is not easily answered. Take one such example from "The Future of India" in which he took to task 'the non-Brahmin castes' and held them responsible for their own plight.

> Who told you to neglect spirituality and Sanskrit learning? What have you been doing all this time? Why have you been indifferent? Why do you now fret and fume because somebody else had more brains, more energy, more pluck and go than you?. . . The moment you do these things you are equal to the Brahmin. (298)

In the praise of his land and religion he speaks in the vein of Pericles who spoke in "The Praise of Athens." In disseminating Shri Ramakrishna's teachings he is modern prototype of St. Paul who was the first apostle of Christ. As Demosthenes exhibited his persuasiveness in politics, Vivekananda showed this skill in religion and in a short time he could make more than three thousand disciples in the West. Demosthenes in his speech, "The Danger of Appeasement," creates the motion and tension through his conditional sentences—"If you chose to follow his example and profess that you are at peace, I raise no objection." It is popular even today in political oratory but now it serves more the diabolical purposes of the politicians. But in Vivekananda it is positive, simple and hypothetical as for example "If Vedanta . . . spreads, the whole humanity will become spiritual."

Like a Ramist, he has a strong leaning towards the immediacy of warmth of the poetic argument but he does not conceive an argument like a Ramist simply as an image or term. Both have a strongly practical system in that they stress examples more than theory. But Vivekananda does not let his oratory become artificial. His oratory has the burning flame of Satan's undaunted resolution and a sense of urgency. Milton disliked oratory and therefore his God is rightly devoid of rhetorical power. Intrestingly enough it is the character of Satan that appeals to Vivekananda the most in the *Paradise Lost.* But oratory as a form of literature has never died out, it has continued in one form or another—in the oratorical speeches of fictitious characters—say in Brutus, Antonio or in the superb parody of *Pickwick Papers* or in the law court, Parliament, on public pulpit—sometimes effulgent, at others subdued. However, the scientific spirit gradually began to gain ground in this genre. By the nineteenth century the scientific spirit pervaded all forms of art and literature. Moreover, the eighteenth century with its prime orators, the Younger Pitt and Charles, James Fox, Edmund Bruke and Sheridan who dazzled the 'best club in England' with their carefully polished brilliance and the nineteenth century with its preacher Newman, orators like William Thackeray (*The Four Georges*), John Ruskin, Victor Hugo, Randolph Churchill maintained the sanctity of oratory. Vivekananda, born and brought up in an atmosphere charged with Victorian spirit, was influenced in his oratory in one way or another by the Victorian orators and preachers. That is why he makes a scientific, psychological and humanistic interpretation of Vedanta philosophy. He is perhaps the most analytic, eclectic and scientific of all modern preachers. He has the dramatic power and sincerity of Newman. He argues like him exploring arguments with gentle insistence so as to show the self-contradictions of his opponents. His introspective honesty and controlled irony, the modulated flow of his prose, the assimilation of a scientific spirit in his religious discourses put him among the Victorian preachers. His Movement is identical, in some respects, to the contemporary Oxford Movement in England. Both aimed at reviving their respective religions from their state of decadence in which they had fallen. Like Carlyle, he preached renunciation, work and hero-worship. But Swamiji's heroes were the two extremes—the incarnations and the downtroddens while Carlyle's heroes were prophets, kings, poets, aristocrats and the likes. Swamiji, though no less thrilling, convincing and persuasive in the art of oratory than the modern speakers like Winston Churchill, Roosevelt and Nehru, could not get the same popularity and recognition in the literary and public field. It is partly due to the lack of modern facilities. A.N. Gilkes and R.H. Ellingworth in the 'Introduction' to *An Anthology of Oratory* rightly comments: "A new technique was required, and a great new age of oratory arose; . . . Able now to call the world on the air preachers, statesman and philosophers have eagerly and often magnificently, grasped the opportunity. Without the radio Churchill could not have roused the 'buoyant and imperturable temper' of Britain nor created the mood he did so much to express." (6)

And partly because he is subjected to 'Indian misfortune.' Vivekananda was conscious of it and termed it as superstition. He used to say that "If a man quotes . . . a Huxley, a Tyndall, or a Darwin it is swallowed without salt." We recognized him as a prophet and philosopher only when the West gave him recognition. Hardly any serious attempt has been made to study the literary value of his speeches and writings. One may well ask if we are waiting for an English critic to give him recognition in that way.

His craftsmanship is evident in the skilful change of style. Usually, he speaks in a simple colloquial and Senecan style. Whenever he turns to India's glorious heritage of her ancient sages and impersonal scriptures, his style becomes grand and sublime to suit the grand theme. Take for example the first sentence of "The Future of India": "This is the ancient land where wisdom made its home before it went into any other country, the same India whose influx of spirituality is represented, as it were, on the material plane, by rolling rivers like oceans, where the eternal Himalayas, rising tier above tier with their snow-caps, looks as it were, into the very mysteries of heaven." (*Works*, 3: 235)

The use of phrases like 'influx of spirituality,' 'rolling rivers' with alliteration of 'r' sound; the visual image of 'eternal Himalayas,' 'snow caps' coupled with the mystic feeling of the phrase 'mysteries of heaven' in this periodical sentence with swift rhythmic movement gives an effect of sublimity and grandiloquence. In many other passages the sublimity and elegance of style is achieved by the use of Sanskrit phrases and words taken from scriptures and through metaphors and similes.

He believes that 'the very sound of Sanskrit words gives a prestige and a power and a strength to the raçe.' The same can be applied to literature. For example we may cite the first sentence of his lecture at Calcutta "The Vedanta in All Its Phases," that is in some respects akin to the earlier citation:

> Away back where no recorded history, nay, not even the dim light of tradition can penetrate, has been steadily shining the light, sometimes dimmed by external circumstances, at others effulgent, but undying and steady, shedding its lustre not only over India, but permeating the whole thought world with its power, silent, unperceived, gentle, yet omnipotent, like the dew that falls in the morning, unseen and unnoticed, yet bringing into bloom the fairest of roses: this has been the thought of the Upanishads, the philosophy of the Vedanta. (*Works*, 3: 322)

This is reminiscent of Ciceronian style that seems rather unusual from an orator who has been speaking or writing in the West in pithy sentences in the Baconian style. The recurrent use of adjective followed by a simile (dew) that stands for the world, culminating into the metaphor the 'fairest of roses and the tracing of the origin of Vedanta philosophy from the prehistoric period give it an air of grandiloquence and sublimity.

Again, to draw the attention of the audience and to give a personal authenticity to the contents he uses the term 'mark you' and 'believe me' in almost all speeches in this group but he never uses these terms in the West. Perhaps it is due to the familiarity and intimacy with the audience.

As for the device of repetition—whatever form it takes, and whether simple repetition or repetition with a difference—it is a powerful weapon in Vivekananda's oratory which can be easily noticed in most of his speeches. Again, he frequently employs repetition of letters, words and aphorisms to achieve memorability and 'punch.' Another type of repetition is the repetition of subject. His principal subject is the teachings of Vedanta combined with the concept of *Daridranarayana* that runs through almost all the pages of his works—be it his oratory, prose writings, poems or letters. He repeats the main idea in various ways. He wants to impress upon the mind of his audience. An example is 'Vedanta and Indian Life.' When he has to ask Indians to avoid all weakness and get 'strength' by meditating on the nucleus of Vedanta *Aham Brahmasmi*—I am spirit, god,—he repeats the word 'weak' and 'strength' several times. And towards the end of the speech, he repeats the word 'light' nine times in a small paragraph. When he wants to drive home the idea that religion is the backbone of India, in his lecture "The Mission of the Vedanta," he keeps on repeating the word 'religion' and 'spirituality' till the end. In one particular sentence, the word faith occurs five times—"Faith, faith, faith in ourselves, faith, faith in God. This is the secret of greatness." Similar examples occur in his different lectures. One such typical quotation is: *ekam Sat Viprabahudha Vadanti*. Again, we have numerous allusions and references ranging from classical scriptures to modern writers. The Vedas, the Upanishads, the Gita, the Bible, Shri Ramakrishna, Buddha, Christ, Shankara, Ramanuja, Greeks, Romans and Jews are some of the common sources of allusions but they are generally vague and passing ones and not subtle except those which are taken from the Hindu scriptures and the *Bible*.

Vivekananda's narrative power and dramatic skill are at their best when he narrates the story of the *Ramayana*, the *Mahabharata*, *The Story of Jada Bharata* and *The Story of Prahlada* at the Shakespeare Club, California, with a Marthian spell. He appears in them not as a rhetorician but as a story-teller. There is an age-old tradition of story-telling in India in which preachers, grandmothers and fathers tell stories of the *Ramayana* and the *Mahabharata* and other stories from mythology to the children. Swamiji tells the story with all its liveliness and impressiveness. This, nevertheless, does not make him a story-writer or story-teller. If he had lived longer, he might have written stories for he had expressed his longing for writing stories like *Alice in Wonderland.*

Like an accomplished craftsman, he uses metaphor, simile, images, allegory and other figures of speech. His figures are generally functional and the sense is imbued in them. See for example the use of metaphor: "freedom we talk about is the glimpse of the blue sky through the clouds and that the real freedom—the blue sky itself—is behind." (*Works*, 3: 14) The image of 'blue sky' is mainly symbolic and 'its power' resides in the emotional and intellectual complex that it transmits via its sensuous element.

Another example is the tactile image of a 'gigantic tree' that stands for the future of India and this image is supported by 'Urdhvamula'—a Sanskrit image. He draws his images from various sources that range from Indian mythology and literature to the Western literature, and from everyday life to modern science but they are rarely farfetched. Images of 'ocean,' 'snowcaps' 'tidal waves,' 'rock,' 'river,' 'ganga,' 'rose,' etc., animal imagery of 'sheep,' 'bird,' 'lion,' 'lamb,' 'serpent,' 'parrot,' 'dog's curly tail,' 'fish,' 'dogs,' 'monkeys,' etc. not only give colour but help the hearer understand the subtlety of his philosophy. The image of 'screen,' 'the Golden Fleece,' 'Tantalus's hell,' the image of 'light' and 'darkness' are used to illustrate the Vedantic concept of Maya. Again, he uses the image of 'whirlpool' and 'mad monkey' to show the state of human mind. The relation between man and God is driven home by the image of 'waves in the Ocean.' Being a renouncer, he conjures up the images of selflessness—'Gopi' and 'Krishna.' Images drawn from modern science and industry, to name some, are 'silkworm,' 'cocoon,' 'national ship,' 'tornado,' 'Locomotive,' 'worm,' 'bacteria,' 'germs,' etc. We also have some farfetched metaphors drawn from the Upanishads: "The other world, O Gautam is the fire. The sun is its fuel, The rays are smoke. The day is the flame. The moon is the embers. And the stars are the sparks." Vivekananda had a great fascination for the poetry of the Upanishads and he employs the whole range of imagery—concrete and abstract.

As for diction, he introduces a panorama of Vedantic terms, least known to the Western people. And it was an arduous task to translate, explain and imprint these on the minds of the hearers. *Appeal-Avalanche* called his choice of words as 'the gems of the English language.' *Detroit Free Press* enlightens us by its on-the-spot observation:

> This dusky gentleman uses poetical imagery as an artist uses colors, and the hues are laid on just where they belong, the result being somewhat bizarre in effect, and yet having a peculiar fascination. Kaleidoscopic were the swiftly succeeding logical conclusions, and the deft manipulator was rewarded for his efforts from time to time by enthusiastic applause. (*Works*, 3: 497)

But in the treasure of his diction, there was no dearth of words and phrases from the scriptures of other religions like Christians, Jews, Hebrews, Islam, Buddhist, Confucius. His oft-quoted French phrase is *raison d'etre*. However he rarely uses Latin or French words, but Sanskrit and Hindi words and phrases followed by their English translation are common. The wide ranging references, allusions and the choice of connotative words like *Maya*, *Atma*, Soul, Ahur Mazada, nihilism, utilitarianism, materialism, Hegelianism, atheism, *Pran*, cosmic mind, *Satchitananda*, Henotheism, *Purus*, *Jiva* and such numerous words, variation in tone and style according to the need of the subject and occasion, the universality of the subject, systematic arrangement of thought and its artistic presentation—all these and more make his oratory a classic work of literature.

Advaita Vedanta

A great deal of Vivekananda's writings, lectures and discourses concentrate on two subjects: religion and social work. And he has tried to establish a harmony between the two. As Vinoba Bhave said that he synthesized the concept of Vedanta and that of *Daridranarayana*. Elements of Vedanta can be traced in his letters, informal talks and his reply to several Addresses. Religion, as he perceived it, turns out to be the *suo moto* of his lifelong endeavour. And his religion was universal, all-inclusive and practical. It inv.olved the worship of *Daridranarayana* and wiping the tears of the suffering ones all over the world without discriminating among religious institutions, continental boundaries and races. In his very first *Samadhi* at Cossipore, he finds an answer to all the problems of the physical world in the religion of Advaita Vedanta that can reconcile all philosophies.

Advaita Vedanta was not new to India. Vivekananda inherited it in its concrete form from Adi Shankaracharya and saw its practical demonstration in the life of his guru Shri Ramakrishna. Though the system of Advaita Vedanta was given a concrete form and shape by its architect Adi Shankaracharya, it has its origin in the *Vedas*, the *Upanishads* and the *Bhagavad Gita*. According to Vivekananda, this Advaita concept was boldly demonstrated by Lord Buddha much before Shankaracharaya. But Swamiji nowhere refers to Gaudapada who is referred to by M.K. Ventakarama Iyer in *Advaita Vedanta* as the great predecessor of Shankara who prepared the ground for Shankara's Advaita Vedanta in his commentary on the *Manduka Upanishad*. Gaudapada's doctrine of *Nirgun Brahman* and of the philosophy of Maya are the essential features of Advaita Vedanta. However, the *Vedas* and the *Upanishads*, the *Gita* and the Advaita of Shankara remained the main source of the

Advaita of Vivekananda.

Vivekananda exhibited his connoisseurship in exploring evidences of Advaitism in various religious systems including Buddhism and Christianity. Buddha who had refuted the authority of the Vedas is called by him a Vedantic, a preacher of Advaita Vedanta. Again Christianity which is essentially a dualistic religion with its concept of three Gods—God the Father, God the Son and God the Ghost—is looked at from a different angle by Swamiji. He avers that Christ was a non-dualist and what appeared to us dualistic concept of God is only meant for the common masses 'who could not conceive of anything higher than a personal God.' "Pray to your father in heaven" Christ preached it to the commoners but to others he taught "I am the vine, ye are the branches." But when he said, "I and my Father are one," he proclaimed the highest truth about religion and that is the Advaita of Christ. Such discoveries, reinforce Vivekananda's Vedantic concept that Advaita is the underlying current in all religions, that the essentials of all religions are one, that all quarrels among religions are on dualistic plane and the sooner the world realizes it the better it is.

The Vedas are the earliest record of religion and philosophy, assiduously composed in hymns by our Rishis. Confronted by the phenomena of nature like rain, thunder, earthquake, etc., they sought to explain these in terms of their causer because nothing can happen without a cause. These causes were found in the agency of some gods or goddesses. This line of explanation gave birth to Vedic Polytheism, to anthropomorphic gods and goddesses. Gradually, the number of gods and goddesses swelled to an unmanageable extent. Various attempts were made to reduce the number. In this course, our Rishis reasoned out a dualistic notion of God—that there is one Supreme God and others are presiding ones invested with great strength, knowledge and moral excellence. So, this concept of personal god or goddess appealed to the people and is still popular all over the world in one name or another. But later on, the reality, the most sublime vision of God, dawned to the Rishis. This idea is beautifully brought out in one of the mantras of the Rig Veda which declares that Reality is one and that sages call it by different names—*Indra*, *Varun*, *Agni*, etc.

Indram mitram varunam agnim ahuh
Atho divyas sa suparno garutman
Ekam sad vipra bahudha vadanti
Aganim yamam matarisvanam ahuh

The concept of Advaita gradually took a definite shape in the Upanishads which came at the end of each Veda and therefore are known as Vedanta. The *Chandogya Upanishad* asserts "*Tat Tvam Asi*"—'thou art that' or *Jiva* is Brahman. In the *Brihadaranyaka Upanishad*, it is said: *Aham Brahma Asmi*. And so say the *Gita* and other scriptures. These concepts were scattered in rudimentary form here and there which Shankara assimilated and presented before us in its finest form. Later, Swami Vivekananda made it a significant movement in America and Europe. He broadened its scope, embracing different religious and philosophical thoughts that apparently look antagonistic to it and reconciling them into an ever effulgent, scientific, practical, non-destructive, universal philosophy of Advaita Vedanta. Vedantic eclecticism of Swamiji eschewed the orthodox line. And here lies the Romantic element in him. *The Hindustan Standard* of 17 Jan. 1963 writes: "it was Vivekananda who achieved the unity of Advaita and Vedanta." As he proclaims in a lecture "The Necessity of Religion" delivered in London:

> Religion must be studied on a broader basis than formerly. All narrow, limited, fighting ideas of religion have to go. All sect ideas and tribal or national ideas of religion must be given up. . . . The religious ideals of the future must embrace all that exists in the world and is good and great, and, at the same time, have infinite scope for future development. . . . Religions must also be inclusive, and not look down with contempt upon one another, because their particular ideals of God are different. (*Works*, 2: 67)

It is primarily this spirit in Vivekananda that makes him the most modern preacher, relevant to our age, and a distinct and unique saint. Mohammed preached that his holy *Koran* is the only truth. Christ taught us that the only truth is the *Bible*. Buddha refuted all else and gave his own truth. So did the rest. Their religions are based on the dictates of one person and one holy book. Except Buddhists, they not only preached their creeds but forced the others to follow the same by military power. The Mohammedans and the Christians spread their religions by the power of wealth and arms. They call others sinners or *Kafirs*. But Swamiji refused to call any-one a sinner. Rather he called them 'the children of immortal bliss.' Should the 'children of immortal bliss' be tamed and enslaved? Certainly not. It was this unifying spirit in Vivekananda that made him the hero of the Parliament of Religions. From the pulpit of the Parliament, he called upon America "to proclaim to all quarters of the globe that the Lord is in every religion." He declared that Lord is in every created being. And he asked the Christians to re-alize the truth, to shake off their fanaticism and, as William Blake puts it, 'to lean in joy upon our Father's knee.' Some speakers of the Parliament like Prince Serge Wolkonsky, Colonel Thomas, Wentworth Higginson, Lyman Abott, Alfred W. Momerie and H.R. Haweis shared his view and appreciated him. Another speaker Rev-erend E.L. Rexford of Boston truly echoed Vivekananda while read-ing his paper on "The Religious Intent": "No ruthless hand shall justly destroy any form of deity while yet it arrests the reverent mind and heart of man. . . . 'God-consciousness,' to borrow a noble word from Calcutta, has been the goal of them all [religious teach-ers]." (Burke, 1: 120)

It was one facet of the Parliament but usually the delegates were engaged in the 'battle of books' and wits. In that exchange of bitter acrimonies, Vivekananda might have failed to make the hardcore orthodox see reason, though he used all his skills, giving concession to the conservationists while admitting the radicals, ac-cepting both oriental and occidental as truth, praising sometimes, chastising at others. He criticized the pretended charity of the Chris-tian missions in India while inviting the true mission of Christ. He got the acceptance of Bishop Keane who said: "I endorse the denunciation that was hurled forth last night against the system of pretended charity that offered food to the hungry Hindus at the cost of their conscience and faith. It is a shame and a disgrace to those who call themselves Christians." (*Works*, I: 126)

In the Parliament of Religions, Vivekananda left no stone un-turned to bring all religions on one platform, so that a consensus on a universal religion could be arrived at—that could bring 'lilacs out of the dead land' and salvage the East and the West alike from what Eliot calls, 'the brown fog of a winterdawn' and at the same time 'that could wipe the tears of the widow,' that could give material welfare as an aid to spiritual growth to the Asiatic countries, to the needy ones. "And such a religion exists," writes Romain Rolland, "it is the Advaita of India, Non-Dualism, Unity, the idea of the Absolute, of the Impersonal God, 'the only religion that can have any hold on intellectual people.'" (259) Though Vivekananda got little success in his immediate mission to the West on both fronts, religious and economic, he sowed the seeds of Advaita there and formed a different image of India as a spiritual leader. Today Advaita is the most popular of all Vedantic schools in America. Swamiji's work is still continuing all over the world.

To make a true assessment of Advaita and its relevance, we have to study the Advaitic concept of *Maya*, cosmology and God in relation with the dualistic systems. Vivekananda's conclusion is that man is so enveloped in the mist of senses that he has forgotten his real identity: "But there is the real existence in and through every thing and that reality, as it were, is caught in the meshes of time, space and causation. There is the real man, the infinite, the beginningless, the endless, the ever-blessed, the ever-free." (*Works*, 2: 32)

The appearance of infinite as finite is Maya. Maya is not a hypothesis but 'a statement of fact.' That the reality of things is different from their outward appearance is Maya. M.K.V. Iyer illustrates the concept of Maya by giving the example of 'a straight stick [that] appears bent in water,' 'To the passengers in a moving train, the trees appear to be moving in opposite direction,' and avers that Advaita Vedanta attributes such phenomena to our inherent limitations that come close to the theory of Physical Science. The disparity between appearance and reality is caused by the inherent limitations in our sensory and intellectual apparatus. According to modern science, the sensations which impinge upon our sense organs lack colour, temperature, sound and texture and these qualities are imposed on the sensations by the mind. Edington says, 'The mind weaves an impression out of the stimuli travelling along the nerves to the brain. The notion of a substance possessing the attributes of colour and sound is a pure mental concept.' (Qtd. Iyer, 1964: 67) He goes on to say that epistemological consideration accounts for our inability to know things as they are. What our sense terminals receive is the stimulation given to them by photons operating within the frequencies which the particular sense organ is adapted to receive. The human eye for example can distinguish light rays only within certain wavelength limits. Thus Edington challenged the claim of complete objectivity in the study of physics. Swamiji anticipates it when he says:

> They [the Vedic thinkers] made some of the grandest generalizations that have yet been reached, and some still remain as theories, which modern science has yet to get even as theories. For instance they not only arrived at the ether theory, but went beyond and classified mind also as a still more rarefied ether. Beyond that again, they found a still more rarefied ether. Yet that was no solution, it did not solve the problem. No amount of knowledge of the external world could solve the problem. (*Works*, 2: 90)

He anticipates Edington's conclusion but goes beyond M.K.V. Iyer's illustration of 'a stick appears bent in water.' Science has solved it by giving the theory of refraction of light—actually, it is an illusion. Maya is not an illusion. Maya is real as far as this world of senses is concerned. But how can science explain such contradictions in life as illustrated by Swamiji in his lecture "Maya and Illusion" delivered in London in October 1896. We know that the bondage is ephemeral yet we cling to it. 'Each day thousands are dying,' 'still men think they will never die.' The good of one is bad for another. The prosperity of one depends upon the misfortune of another. The knowledge of happiness brings the knowledge of unhappiness. He cites some more illustrations. The oldest idea of Maya however, Swamiji admits, is the sense of delusion illustrated in one of the Vedas and in the *Avetasvatara Upanishad*: "Know nature to be Maya and the Ruler of this Maya is the Lord Himself." (*Works*, 2: 88-89)

If we accept it, then Maya and the Lord become two entities, two Realities. And the ruler, as a matter of fact, cannot be impersonal or *Nirgun*. So this Vedic idea, if taken for granted, kills the very concept of Advaita Vedanta. See how easily Vivekananda clears this contradiction:

> The idea of a personal God, the Ruler, and Creator of this universe, as He has been styled, the Ruler of Maya of nature, is not the end of these Vedantic ideas; it is only the beginning. The idea grows and grows until the Vedantist finds that he who, he thought, was standing outside, is he himself and is in reality within. He is the one who is free, but who through limitation thought he was bound. (*Works*, 2: 104)

Looked at with an eye of intellect, *Maya*, *Jiva* and *Brahman* appear distinct. But the touch of Reality effaces all these contradictions and distinctions. Till then, we have to move through these tremendous contradictions, fighting against nature of Maya.

Nyaya system and Buddhist concept come to somewhat the same conclusion of the limitation of mind. According to the Buddhists, the mental interpretation of *Svalaksanas* in terms of *Jati*, *Kriya*, *Guna* and *Sambandha* distorts them. It may do well to recall how Kant, taking the same position, interprets that it is the mind that imposes the notions of time, space and cause in the indeterminate sensations. That is why all mystics of the world opine that the only way is to transcend mind and come to superconscious state, that is Samadhi. Wordsworth beautifully describes this state of consciousness in "Tintern Abbey":

> Is lightened: that serene and blessed mood,
> In which the affections gently lead us on,
> Until the breath of this corporeal frame
> And even the motion of our human blood
> Almost suspended, we are laid asleep
> In body, and become a living soul.

It is only there that the veil of Maya lifts from the world and the truth becomes apparent. And what one perceives at this *Nirvikalpa Samadhi* is *Nirgun Brahman*. As Shankaracharya said:

Maya-Pancharatnam,
Nirupamanityaniramsake apyakande
Mayi citisarvikalpanadi sunye
Chatavati Jagadisa jivabhedam (*Works*, 16: 209)

The concept of God in the Advaita is the culmination of a long evolution in the concept of God. Vivekananda gives a lively account of this evolution in his lecture "Maya and the Concept of God." The history of this evolution dates back to the origin of man. Men tried to idealize gods, for physical power was not enough. The idea of ruthless Jehovah in the *Old Testament* or the indecent behaviour of Indra was no more acceptable to the later generation. Men's inquiring spirit gave birth to anthropomorphic gods and goddesses in whom they found the cause of natural phenomena. In this way, man's idea of God kept on changing and expanding until he reached its apex in the Advaita philosophy. Through the various doctrines, says Vivekananda, runs the golden thread of unity; and it is the purpose of the Vedanta to discover this thread: "the thread that runs through all these various ideas, each one of these like a pearl, says the Lord Krishna."

Vivekananda recognised it in its true spirit and could see the boldest pronouncement of Advaita even in the doctrine of no-God, the atheism of Buddhism and Jainism. Lord Buddha did not believe in the existence of God but the Buddhists made him God. In Jainism, there is no personal God but all liberated souls are regarded as gods. Let us see how young Narendra and his master react to the word atheist:

Narendra: He [Buddha] could not express in words what he had realized by his spiritual practices; so people say he was an atheist.

Master: Why atheist? He was not an atheist. He simply could not express his inner experiences in words. Do you know what 'Buddha' means? It is to become one with Bodha, Pure Consciousness. It is to become Pure Consciousness itself. (*Works*, I: 175)

The real Buddha, according to Nagarjuna, must be perceived

directly by mystic intuition. Thus there comes to be a world of two realities: the *Samvriti Satya* and the *Parinispanna Satya*, Not-Being and Being in Parmenides, Opinion and Truth in Plato, Appearance and Reality in Bradley, Intellect and Intuition in Bergson or Thisness and Thatness in Buddhism. R.D. Ranade calls Buddha 'a Pracchanna Advaitin.' He calls Nagarjuna and Gaudapada as "the off-shoot of Sceptico-mystical' tendency. But in Swamiji one finds both Sceptico-mystical and 'logicodialectical tendency.'

The term God is perhaps the most controversial, most debated in the realm of religion and philosophy. The Jain philosophers and the agnostics pose a volley of questions—Is God knowable? If God is infinite how does infinite become finite? Has he qualities? G.B. Shaw in *The Revolutionist's Handbook* echoes this controversy and urges for the necessity of God:

> If there were no God, said the eighteenth century Deist, it would be necessary to invent him. Now this XVIII century God was *deus ex machina*, the god who helped those who could not help themselves. . . . The nineteenth century decided that there is indeed no such god; and now Man must take in hand all the work that he used to shirk with an idle prayer.

Though Shaw's God and his belief that man is the master of nature seem quite in agreement with those of Swamiji, his God is more than this. The *Bhagavad Gita* gives a very subtle and sublime description of God: "He seems to possess the faculties of all the senses and yet He is devoid of the senses. He is unattached and yet He sustains all things. He is free from the dispositions of nature and yet He enjoys them. He is without and within all beings. He has no movement and yet He moves. He is too subtle to be known. He is far away and yet He is near. He is undivided and yet he is as it were divided among beings. He is to be known as the sustainer of all creation. He devours and generates." (Chap. XIII.14.16)

Shankara and Vivekananda have shared this splendid verse that seems to be built on a pattern of paradoxes. One may ponder for a while: Should God be so paradoxical, so complicated? Certainly not. What seems to be a paradox is the result of two angles of viewing God. The description encompasses both realities: the world of matter and the world of spirit. God is unknowable as one knows an object through senses but more than knowable because it is realizing the self. 'We have to know in Him and through Him.' (*Works*, 2: 133) "He is the eternal subject of everything" (*Works*, 2: 134) and we cannot objectify Him. Strictly speaking, God is without faculties or attributes (*Nirgun*) as realized in superconscious state but if He is looked at through our intellect; He appears with all the attributes that the world possesses (*Sagun*). He is the nearest for He is I (Thou art that) yet farthest for man who tends to look outward rather than inward. M.K.V. Iyer maintains: "Nirguna Brahman is immutable. It does not undergo the least change. What is beyond name and form and consequently *Sui generis* cannot descend to a lower plane and acquire qualities. . . . It is conceived as *Kutastha nitya* (cause) and not *Parinami nitya* (effect)." (*Advaita Vedanta*, 79)

Yet it is Brahma that is evolving in all evolutions without being changed. Swamiji illustrates it by giving a notation in which (a) is the Absolute (b) is the Universe and (c) is time, space and causation. "This Absolute (a) had become the universe (b) through time, space and causation (c)." (*Works*, 2: 130) Thus (c) is like a glass through which (a) appears as (b). In this way, the Advaita solves this apparent contradiction. "The Vedantist," as Swamiji puts it, "gives no other attributes to God except these three—that He is infinite Existence, Infinite Knowledge, and Infinite Bliss, and he regards these three as one. Existence without knowledge and love cannot be; knowledge without love and love without knowledge cannot be. What we want is the harmony of Existence, Knowledge and Bliss Infinite." (*Works*, 2: 143)

Indeed, Swamiji worked all his life to harmonize the seemingly divergent paths of religion. In his Advaita philosophy, he assimilates the vitals of the Hindu, the Christian, the Buddha and the Islam. That is why his Advaita is undestructive. He accepts all religions as truth and criticizes the superstitions in them. He was bold enough to proclaim that if the Sermon on the Mount is truly understood, man would immediately become God. In fact, he understood the teachings of Christ and Buddha better than the Christians and the Buddhists. He claimed, as has been referred before, that Christ was Advaitin: "I and my Father are one." What appears in his teaching, dualistic 'Pray to your Father in Heaven' or the concept of three gods—god the Father, god the Son, god the Ghost—is meant for commoners who cannot understand the Impersonal God. Even when Mohammed preached 'that our Lord is one' and 'I am His prophet,' the Lord was Impersonal and he became the personal god. Buddha preached renunciation and Universal brotherhood. St. Paul reaches the same Advaitic conclusion when he teaches: "Your body is the temple of the holy Ghost which is in You." "Know ye not that ye are the temple of God and that the spirit of God dwelleth in You?" The same is the essence of Judaism that takes man for the image of God, "Ye are gods and all of you are children of the Most High." Much before Swamiji, Ashoka, the Emperor, made an attempt to harmonize all religions as his twelfth edict reads: "He who does reverence to his own sect, while disparaging the sects of other . . . inflicts the severest injury on his own sect." After Ashoka, it was Akbar, the great, who tried to synthesize all religions in his *Din-e-Ilahi*. Sufist movement was also an attempt in the same direction. In this way, the reformers and preachers left behind one path after another but gradually fanaticism got mixed with them. It was the fanaticism in religion that made Swift cry out: "We have just enough religion to make us hate." Swamiji had no conflict with divergent sects. He says that, if we all thought alike, "we would be like Egyptian mummies in a museum, looking at each other without a thought to think." (*Works*, 2: 382) In Swamiji's religion, 'the moralistic philosophy of Buddha,' rationalistic philosophy of Shankara, humanism of Christ and equality and fraternity of Mohammed are embedded. That is why he stresses the need of a universal religion in his lectures time and again. At the Chicago Conference, he calls upon America 'to proclaim to all quarters of the globe that the Lord is in every religion.' 'Paper on Hinduism' read at the Parliament on 19th September 1893 reads: "if there is ever to be a universal religion, it must be one which will have no location in place or time; which will be infinite like the God it will preach, and whose sun will shine upon all the followers of Krishan and of Christ, on saints and sinners alike; which will not be Brahminic or Buddhistic, Christian or Mohammedan, but the sum total of all these." (*Works*, 2: 19) Taking the thread from the Bible, he picks up the concept of *Daridranarayan* and embraces it in his Advaita. Nitish Sengupta, in his article "The First Socialist: Recalling Vivekananda's Journey," believes that the concept of '*Daridranarayan*' 'had its origin in Vivekananda. The author has mistaken the term for concept. Vivekananda might have been the first modern Indian to use the term but certainly he was not its originator. It has its origin in the *Bible* which emphatically asserts that the blessed are those who are meek, poor, for the kingdom of heaven is theirs. The *Bible* debars the rich from entering the heaven. Swamiji does not reject any one but says: "So long as the millions live in hunger and ignorance; I hold every man a traitor who having been educated at their expense pays no heed to them." He exhorts everyone to sacrifice his life for the emancipation of poverty, hunger, illiteracy and backwardness. He reinforces his appeal: "I do not believe in a God who cannot give me bread here agiving me eternal bliss in heaven." He goes to the extent of appealing: "Let the Vedas, the Koran, the Puranas and all scriptural lumber rest now for some time." (*Works*, 6: 410) Again Islam appealed him the most for its social equality among the Muslims. He says that once anyone becomes a Muslim, he is socially equal to even the Caliph of Turkey. His religion includes it but sets no limits of religion or creed and does not call for the murder of nonbelievers as the *Koran* does. In a letter to his friend Sarfaraz Khan, he writes: "How I wish to have in my India an Islamic body with a Vedantic head."

Again, he derives the detailed ideas of Mission work and the active life of a Sannyasin from his Master, Buddhism and Christianity. In India, Sannyasins used to lead a secluded life to get *moksa*. In modern India, he was the first to exhort the monks to make it their mission to alleviate the sufferings of human beings taking them for *Daridranarayana*.

He imbibed all that was good, and gave a positive explanation to all that does not appear good. He realized that what is good today may not be the same tomorrow. The good of one may be bad for another. The science of Ptolemy became a superstition for Copernicus. Therefore, he did not destroy anything; he gave a proper place to everything. The same conclusion is arrived at by Sri Aurobindo Ghose in his book *The Life Divine*: "True reconciliation proceeds always by mutual comprehension leading to some sort of oneness." Again, he writes: "As in science, so in metaphysical thoughts; that general and ultimate solution is likely to be the best which includes and accounts for all, so that each truth, as experience, takes its place in the whole."

His religion is progressive and has infinite space for further accommodation as the time demands. He welcomed the true message of Christ in India but scathingly attacked Christian's and Islam's jingoistic, martial propagation of their religions. The spread of these religions was based on arms. *Saginaw Evening News,* March 22, 1894, reports on his lecture "Religious Harmony": "The Buddhists, the first missionary religion, have double the number of converts of any other religion and they did not use the sword. The Mohammedans used the most force, and they number the least of the three great missionary religions." (*Works*, 2: 482-83)

Vivekananda was against conversion and mere intellectual discussion. He asked for practical realization of religion in his various lectures like "Realization" delivered in London on 29th October: "I always cling to the idea set forth with one voice by Christ, Buddha and the Vedanta, that we must all come to perfection in time" (*Works*, 2: 174) and exhorted us to try to attain this realization. In the "Practical Vedanta," he showed us that 'there is very little difference between the pure religion of Christ and that of Vedanta' and asked to realize our 'real self' by killing our little self. The same is echoed by Mansur al Hallaj who in his *Mystical Dimensions of Islam* writes:

> Uqtuluni ya thiquati-inna fi quatlinayati
> (Kill me, O my trustworthy friends, for in my being killed is my life).

He takes the sum total of all souls for God, the very existence is God. The function of religion is to realize that 'I am spirit' not body. And once you know yourself, all difference of caste, religion or race disappear. In his lectures on "The Way to the Realization of a Universal Religion," and "The Ideal of Universal Religion," we have his same concern to harmonize the world by showing that essential truth is the same everywhere. Marie Louise Burke rightly assesses his 'prophetic mission' in these words:

> Almost immediately after the beginning of 1895 Swamiji embarked with full vigour and full assurance upon his world mission, that of teaching Vedanta as he conceived it—a religion and philosophy that would suit all different temperaments and different stages of religious development and yet meet man's highest spiritual needs; a religion and philosophy, also, that could be practical in every walk of life, that would be of benefit to every aspect of human existence and would solve such problems as the conflicts between science and religion, utilitarianism and mysticism. (376)

He gave recognition even to material worship but called it the lowest form. Man moves from material worship to mental worship and from mental to spiritual worship as Vedanta philosophy moves from dualistic to qualified nondualistic (Visistadvaita) and from Visistadvaita to Advaita. In his letter to Alasinga on May 6, 1895, Vivekananda rightly calls it 'his discovery.'

It would be interesting to see how Vivekananda reached out a synthesis between science and religion. Being charged with Victorian spirit, he put even religion to the test of science to see if religion can be justified by the 'same methods of investigation which we apply to science.' He was the first Indian Yogi to propagate his findings of the rationalistic investigation in the study of religion all over the world in an international language (English). So firm was his 'intellectual faith' in reason that he declared in England in the lecture "Reason and Religion":

> If a religion is destroyed by such investigations, it was then all the time useless, unworthy superstition; and the sooner it goes the better. . . . Not only will it be made scientific—as scientific, at least, as any of the conclusions of physics or chemistry—but will have greater strength, because physics or chemistry has no internal mandate to vouch for its truth, which religion has. (*Works*, 1: 367)

He develops his idea further by saying that in the 'battle of books' the *Gita*, the *Bible*, the *Koran*, the *Zenda Avasta*, the *Tripitak*—who will be the judge? Certainly it should be reason. In the principle of reasoning, "the particular is explained by the general and the general by the more general until we come to the universal." (*Works*, I: 369) The same method can be employed in religion. The second principle of science is that 'the explanation of everything comes from inside it.' Does force of gravitation lie anywhere else? No, it lies in the earth itself. The law of evolution tells the same thing. These two principles of science, we can very well apply to the study of religion. As for the generalization, our Vedic Rishis have made a number of generalizations and the most sublime of them is the theory of existence. Darwin's theory of evolution falls short to the Vedic theory of evolution. For it tells us that each evolution is preceded by an involution and in this way the cycle goes on. Does the concept of *Dasa Avatar* not give us an evolutionary theory of the world? The *Bible* and the Vedanta both affirm the evolution of creation from word and identify word with God. The Gospel according to John says: "In the beginning was word; word was with God; and word was God." The *Koran* opens with these words:

> Recite thou, in the name of thy Lord.
> Who created:
> Created man from CLOTS OF BLOOD (Rodwell, 19)

So here again we find that the creation of man was due to "CLOTS OF BLOOD" or protoplasm in the scientific terms. Modern science has proved the essential unity of things in the universe—that the universe is composed of matter in its three forms—gas, liquid and solid. Whatsoever the scientific terminology, the essential unity, the oneness of the universe has been proved beyond doubt by almost all religions.

Lucretius in his "Nature of the Universe" said that invisible atoms were the cause of the universe:

> I will reveal those atoms from which nature creates all things and increases and feeds them and into which, when they perish, nature again resolves them. To these in my discourse I

> commonly give such names as the 'raw material' or 'generative bodies' of 'seeds' of things. Or I may call them 'primary particles,' because they come first and everything else is composed of them.

We are also reminded of Goethe who writes in his poem "West Eastern Devan" (based on the *Koran*):

> God's in the East!
> God's in the West!
> North and South and every land
> Lie in the calm peace of His Land!

The first two lines have been taken from the holy *Koran*. The same concept of oneness we have in the *New Testament*. The *Upanishad* and the *Gita* stress it again and again. In Nyaya philosophy we find five proofs for the existence of God: (i) Cosmological proof (ii) Logical proof (iii) Udayana's proof by experiment (iv) Moral proof (v) Vatsyayana's intuitive proof.

It is beyond the scope of the present chapter to go into details of these but one thing is certain: except intuitive proof others are based more or less on reason. Of course everyone has to admit the limitations of reason. By reason one may prove a religious concept but one cannot realize the goal of religion—'Know thy self.' R.D. Ranade writes: "The Sutras II 1.11, 1.1.3, III.2.24, are definitive on this point. The first three Sutras constitute the three main criteria for God. The first Sutra speaks of reason, the second of revelation and the third of intuition." And finally comes the knowledge of the self. Thomas Browne also says that he carried his reason to its 'O altitudo' yet mysteries remain. It shows that Browne, himself a doctor, had realized the limitation of reason. We see that in religion we have to begin with disbelief and move from reason to revelation to the intuition as we move from consciousness to unconsciousness to superconsciousness or as we move from the personal to the general to the Universal. Swamiji called it more scientific than any other science for it is going inward—the study of the self. The science of religion invites one to realize the truth oneself. It gives us a definite system to follow and anybody can see the result. Swamiji called upon the people not to believe in God until you see God and hence it appeals even to the atheist. His *Summum bonum* of religion lies in it:

> Each soul is potentially divine. The goal is to manifest this Divinity within by controlling nature, external and internal. Do this either by work, or worship, or psychic control, or philosophy—by one, or more, or all of these—and be free. This is the whole of religion. Doctrines, or dogmas, or rituals, or books, or temples, or forms, are but secondary details. (*Works*. 1: 124)

Swamiji, in his four treatises *Karma-Yoga*, *Bhakti-Yoga*, *Raja-Yoga*, *Jnana-Yoga*, prescribes the method of reaching the Infinite. It is, however, not possible for everyone to follow the path of Yoga. In that case, one has to rely on *aptwakya*—the words of a Buddha. So is the case with science. As long as you have not felt for yourself how one feels on the moon or in the space, you rely on a Neil Armstrong or a Yuri Gagrin. Swamiji has commented on several science theories like the one of genetics. He explodes the myth of genetic inheritance. He rejects the claim that man inherits everything through genes and goes on to prove that another source of inheritance is the previous life. As about energy, Swamiji claims that "all the various forms of cosmic energy, such as matter, thought, force, intelligence, and so forth, are simply the manifestations of that cosmic intelligence. (*Works*, 2: 211) This concept of 'cosmic intelligence' appeals to science. "The chief difference," according to Romain Rolland, "is that with science it remains a piece of mechanism, while Vivekananda breathes life into it," Further, he records his impression: "And the reasoning of a religious and learned man like Vivekananda does not seem to me very different in scientific quality from that 'Logic of the Infinite.'" (262)

It is this 'grand symphony,' as Gautam Sen phrased it, between science and religion, oriental and occidental, heresy and orthodoxy, material and spiritual world, dualistic, Visist Advaita and Advaita that makes him relevant to our age and his teachings time-immemorial.

To him, "religion is the science of the spirit, the soul, the science of life, and the science of being." He fully comprehended

Shri Ramakrishna's saying: "The Moghul coins have no currency under the East India Company's rule." The religion of the medieval age is not fit for the modern age and hence has to be scientific. About the basic law of religion, he says: "As mathematics in every part of the world does not differ, so the mystics do not differ. They are all similarly constituted and similarly situated. Their experience is the same, and this becomes law."

In his Advaita philosophy, he deals at length with the cosmological problems and their answers that he finds in his scriptures and their affinity at several points with the views of science on them. He refutes the dualistic notion that some personal God created the whole universe. The *Bible* and the *Koran* hold that the Lord Himself created everything. This notion works against the evolutionary theory and hence is unscientific. The dualists in India and elsewhere hold the same view. But the Advaita philosophy proves most scientific. The universe is infinite in time and space. We do not know when it began or when it will end. Of course, the human conception of the universe has been changing with the passage of time. When the universe was first conceived of as an orderly unit, it was called cosmos. Today we call it space and its study space-science. Numerous attempts have been made to know its mysteries by the philosophers, yogis and by the astronomers. Among the philosophers, Sankhya, Vaisesika, Buddhists, Jains and Vedantists and among the astronomers, Ptolemy and Copernicus made the most significant contribution to it. After Copernican theory, several new theories have come up but mysteries about the universe remain. Dr. Jackburns, Associate Astronomy Professor at the University of New Mexico, says: "The biggest unanswered question in Astronomy is whether the universe will keep expanding or whether the entire universe will begin contracting down into what some people have called a big crunch." (Manorama Year Book 1986, 68) It is an immutable law of nature that there must be a cause for everything. "Nothing will come of nothing." (*King Lear*, 29) So there must be a cause for the existence of the world. What is it? Advaita Vedanta believes that Brahman, what Swamiji calls 'cosmic intelligence,' is the cause of the world or cosmos. A Sankhya Philosopher may ask: how can *Brahman* that is infinite, pure and homogeneous in nature become the world that is finite, impure and heterogeneous?

Sankhya school of philosophy concludes that *Prakriti* is the cause, and it is the uncaused purusha of all known also as *Avykta* and the world is the manifested effect. The world and its objects can dissolve into their original form *Prakriti* since *Prakriti* is composed of three *gunas: Sattva, Rajas* and *Tamas*, it can evolve into the heterogeneous world through various evolutes such as *Buddhi* (intellect), *Ahamkara* (ego principle) and the *Tanmatras* (subtle elements).

Sankhya has probably not taken into account the true nature of the world. The world looks heterogeneous and finite through senses but is homogeneous, infinite and one. The *Veda* says, "By knowing one lump we know the universe." In his commentary on *Brahma-Sutras* (1.5-11), Shankara says that the non-sentient *Prakriti* cannot perform the act of seeing which, as the *Chandogya Upanishad* (VI and 3) affirms, was performed by the Brahman in order 'to become many and to produce.' If *Prakriti* is independent God, what will be the position of God? A mere figurehead?

Swamiji deals with Sankhya philosophy in his two lectures; "A Study of the Sankhya Philosophy" and "Sankhya and *Vedanta*." His objection to it is on two accounts. How can *Prakriti* that is matter cause the universe without any guiding intelligence, *Purusha*? Secondly, "how can there be more than one *Purusha*. If there are two infinites, they will limit each other and will cease to be infinites. Nevertheless, Swami gives credit to him for constructing 'a building' and the need is to give only a finishing touch. In fact, Sankhya philosophy requires what R.D. Ranade calls 'the background of Purusha in order that evolution of Prakriti takes place.

Among the earliest Indian philosophers, Vaisheshikas seem to be most unscientific. According to the Vaisheshika philosophy, the creation of all physical objects is caused by the combination in different proportions of the four kinds of Paramanus (atoms): earth, water, fire and air. They are indivisible, eternal and uncaused. R.D. Ranade neatly summarizes it in these words: "In short matter in the form of atoms which possess qualities of their own, the pull of the Adrishta, and a push only at start by God, is all the atomic theory of the Vaisheshikas wants in order to explain the origination of the several objects in the world and the emergence or epigenesis of new qualities in them." (*Advaita Vedanta*)

This doctrine is also found wanting in several respects. It is difficult to prove that earth, water, air and fire were uncaused. Even if we accept it, how can cosmic intelligence (God) be guided by unintelligent *Adrishta*? What is the position of God after giving the push? Equally absurd is their doctrine of epigenesis in destruction, especially when it is applied to an organism. Their assumption that cell dies first and next the body is disapproved by science.

In Buddhism, metaphysics and cosmology are least developed. Buddha, though least interested in them, believes in the theories of *Nairatmya* (negative) and *Samghata* (positive) sides of phenomenalistic metaphysics. But how *Samghata* that is phenomenal becomes *Sanatan* (noumenal) does not make much sense. Again his 'ethico-cosmological' theory of the concatenations of twelve causes (*Pratitya-Samutpad*) fails to give any satisfactory solution to the cosmological problem. Buddha repudiates permanence in cosmology but validates it in spiritual knowledge. An Advaitin like Swamiji, however, would appreciate Buddha when he asserts: "I shall continue to be in the future, permanent, immutable eternal of a nature that knows no change." (Majjhim Nikya, 1, 138) It shows the permanence of soul, self, spirit or 'I' or by whatsoever name you may call it. Then now can he deny the permanence in cosmology or the existence of soul?

Jains like Vaisheshikas propounds that the cosmos is the result of the combination of four atoms. Vaisheshikas's atoms are different in quality but Jains's are similar in kind but different in quantity and weight. The combination of atoms takes place due to the humidity or dryness of the combing atoms. Thus it safely does away with God. Science, matter and spirit are distinct in Jainism. So there is no interaction between them. Neither has it a central *monad* as in Leibnitz to regulate atoms. All these theories basically take into account the material cause and leave out the efficient cause.

Naturally then we turn to the Vedanta that provides the best suitable solution. It completes the Sankhya philosophy by providing a universal *Purusha* and resolves the conflict between the Mimansaka and the Naiyayika by identifying word with God. It may do well to recall that the Mimansa upholds the supremacy of Word over God and Naiyayika the vice versa. In his study of cosmology, Swamiji makes no claim of originality: "We do not pretend to throw any new light on those all-absorbing problems, but only to put before you the ancient truth in the language of modern times. (*Works*, 2: 213) Let us begin with the beginning. He quotes from *Rig Veda*: "When there was neither aught nor naught, when darkness was rolling over darkness, what existed?" The answer given is: "It then existed without vibration (Anedavatam)." (*Works*, 2: 435) Swamiji explains that 'it' was *Prana* in condensed, immobile form. And after a long interval when the *Kalpa* began, it came into motion and is still in a state of rapid expansion. *Prana* is the 'primal energy' and when it combines with *Akasha*, a chain reaction takes place and produces every other element. The relation between *Akasha* and *Prana* is analogous with the relation between body and soul. *Prana* manifests itself through *Akasha*: "The Akasha, acted upon by the repeated blows of Prana, produces Vayu or Vibration. This Vayu vibrates, and the vibrations growing more and more rapid result in friction giving rise to heat, *Tajas*. Then this heat ends in liquefaction, *Apah*. Then that liquid becomes solid . . . and it goes back in exactly the reverse way." (*Works*, 2: 435-36)

And this process continues. So, according to Vedanta, there is a circular motion of involution and evolution. Involution or destruction means 'going back to cause.' It means that the universe is without beginning and end. Nothing is destroyed, nothing is created, only the form is changing although it is eternally unchanging. Brahman or the 'cosmic intelligence' is the material and efficient cause of the universe, and the universe is its effect, and that the cause is not different from the effect. This advaitic concept anticipates the general concept of steady state theory advanced by two astronomers Thomas Gold and Hermann Bondi. According to this theory, galaxies recede from one another but their spatial density remains constant. These new galaxies are formed from new matter which is being continuously created to replace old matter which is being dispersed. When Swamiji tells us that at first *Prana* was in a highly condensed state, does he not echo what modern theory of the universe assumes that 'our universe started out as a superdense ball'? Neither Metaphysics nor Astronomy can measure its density or give the precise time table of the changes.

One may well ask what the purpose of God was to manifest himself into the World. To this question Shankaracharya and

Ramakrishna Paramhansa put forward their mystical exclamation that it is merely His *Lila*, sport. Shankaracharya, however, develops his metaphysics that was incorporated long after him by Swamiji. But Ramakrishna ends all mysteries by attributing everything to His *Lila*. Swamiji, here, perhaps transcends his master for the sceptical world is not going to be convinced by the aphorism *Lila*. Swamiji's answer is: "Nature is undergoing all these changes for the development of the soul; all this creation is for the benefit of the soul, so that it may be free. This immense book which we call the universe is stretched out before man so that he may read; and he discovers eventually that he is an omniscient and omnipotent being." (*Works*, 2: 439) And what we see around the world with all its objects has no absolute existence. It exists only in relation to our senses. What exists there is the 'I,' the eternal. That is why some European philosophers claim that "this world exists because I exist."

So far, we have been concentrating on the macrocosm—the external world. However alluring this outward travel may be, we cannot afford to ignore the fundamental principle of the *Vedas*: "that our search in the stars, the nebulae, Milky way, in the whole of this external universe leads to nothing, never solves the problem of life and death. The wonderful mechanism inside had to be analyzed, and it revealed to them the secret of the universe." (*Works*, 2: 439) We have to anatomise our soul. It is a very difficult journey. We have to travel in the reverse gear from macrocosm to microcosm. There have always been several mind boggling questions. What is death? Is there something which survives after death? And if not, what is its destiny? In death what goes out of the body?

Swamiji, in his lecture in New York on the subject "The Cosmos: The Microcosm," refers to body as 'external body' and 'the gross body'—the soul is beyond them. Following the Baconian inductive method, he elucidates subtly what is behind our senses. Eyes, ear, tongue, nose and skin are only external instruments for carrying the sensation inward to the centre. The whole process of receiving the message from the external instruments and sending back to them can be diagrammatically illustrated in this way

E ——> O ——> M ——> I ——> S

E <—— O <—— M <—— I <—— S

in which 'E' is external instrument, 'O' is organ, 'M' is mind, 'I' is intellect and 'S' is soul. 'E' 'O' 'M' are just carriers, 'I' is determining faculty but the final order is given by 'S'. Soul is the ruler of the body. The external body perishes in a few years: "the finer body is not so easily perishable, yet it sometimes degenerates, and at others becomes strong" but soul does not decay. He goes on to say that "when the body is vigorous, the mind becomes vigorous." (*Works*, 2: 215) Swamiji has, however, not mentioned that mind has a greater bearing on the body than the body on the mind. And mind remains alive for sometime even after the death of body. And soul casts off this body and puts on another body as man does with the clothes. Osho Rajneesh says, "there is no death as such. Death is the great illusion, because it always happens to the other; it never happens to you, so you always see it from the outside. You don't know what is happening *inside* at the very innermost centre. Something tremendously valuable is happening there, but all that you know is that the man cannot speak, cannot breathe, cannot walk, . . . he is dead." (62)

In fact we get the perception of a thing through our senses but senses cannot help us in knowing the inner world. Hume in one way and Heidegger in another maintain that the self remains inaccessible to thought. Rajneesh prescribes the course of mediation that is only one step in Raja-Yoga. One can know the soul, the real self, through meditation, nay through Yoga. Vivekananda wrote four treatises on Yoga. In his lecture 'The Cosmos,' he proceeds through logic. He himself raises the question, "How can we know that?" and proves it logically. He says that 'self-illuminating' knowledge cannot belong to the body, dead matter, for that which is self-luminous does not wane. Moon shines through the reflection of sun-light. "Therefore the light which shines through the mind is not its own. Whose is it then? It must belong to that which has its own essence." (*Works*, 2: 216) The knowledge of man has only a relative existence and that which is relative is only reflective. This 'self-luminous' existence is called soul, God, spirit etc. Call it by whatsoever name, but it must be knowledge, existence and blessedness itself. It has neither beginning nor end.

The natural conclusion of this soul theory will be that each one has a soul. How many souls that would be? And if soul is God, how will one reconcile it with the theory of one God with the same attributes propounded in Judaism, Christianity, Islam and even in Hinduism? The theory of one God appears childish to Rajneesh. We are an indivisible part of the cosmos. The soul or God encompasses us all. The material world is the wave in the ocean. So its waves are also ocean but ocean is not wave.

Then Vivekananda moves on to the question of reincarnation. He, like most other mystics, believes in the reincarnation of the soul. Rajneesh also believes in the rebirth of man but refutes the incarnation of God because he denies the separate existence of God and comes close to the Advaitic concept when he puts emphasis on realizing the divinity within. Vivekananda's assessment, to use Lear's words in *King Lear*, is: "Nothing will come of nothing" and hence "we have been existing eternally, and will exist." (*Works*, 2: 217) So even after the death of the body, the soul "rolls round in earth's diurnal course," says Wordsworth in "A Slumber Did My Spirit Seal."

Vivekananda answers the objection raised against it and then puts forward rational proofs. The greatest objection has been why we do not remember our past. In response to it, he puts a counter question: "Do we remember all our past in this life?" (*Works*, 2: 218) If not, should we deny the existence of our babyhood? So the very question is childish. He, however, says that one can recall his previous life and many a man have done it. At Chicago conference, while reading his "Paper on Hinduism," he challenged the scientists to prove it. Our Rishis have done it and have prescribed the method. Swamiji and Rajneesh have laid emphasis on 'knowing the self.' By 'knowing the self,' one knows everything. He further argues: "The latest scientific men are coming back to the ancient sages, . . . They admit that each man and each animal is born with a fund of experience, and that all these actions in the mind are the result of past experience." (*Works*, 2: 221) But the problem lies ahead. Science concludes that man receives only through 'hereditary transmission.' Vivekananda accepts the challenge and goes on to prove that it is a superstition of science. He makes his position clear: "We, by our past actions conform ourselves to a certain birth in a certain body, and the only suitable material for what body comes from the parents who have made themselves fit to have that soul as their offspring." (*Works*, 2: 222)

His first objection to the theory of heredity is that the mental experience cannot be recorded materially. Then he pleads that by transmitting impressions and qualities, the parents should lose that part and their "minds should become vacuum." But that does not happen. Nevertheless, one finds oneself in agreement with Swamiji when he challenges it on this account:

> Again, if in the bioplasmic cell the infinite amount of impressions from all time has entered, where and how is it? This is a most impossible position, and until these physiologists can prove how and where those impressions live in that cell, and what they mean by a mental impression sleeping in the physical cell, their position cannot be taken for granted. (*Works*, 2: 222-23)

Although re-birth or past life is a subjective experience at transcendental state of consciousness, it seldom comes to a man. It cannot be denied unless the existence of soul, God or, in Shaw's words, *Life Force* is denied. The negation of rebirth is the negation of soul, divinity within and infinite existence. And devoid of divinity, man would have no hope for what Bergson calls *elan vital* or creative evolution. It would be the most absurd concept of man. It is a limitation of science that it can study only three states of consciousness out of four mentioned in the Mandukya Upanishad—waking, dream, sleep and transcendental consciousness called *turiya*. Recently some scientists in Moscow discovered that mind has infinite potential and successfully transmitted message to a person living in another place only through deep concentration. With this, one can hope that the time will come when science will reach the same conclusion which Dr. S. Radhakrishnan arrives at in his 'Introduction' to *The Brahma Sutra*:

> Personality is not merely body and mind but spirit, and spirit, as we have seen, is. It is the primal reality more authentic than anything reflected in the objective world. *Atman* is the foundation of the ego, the kernel of the personality. It is the

> universal self active in every ego even as it is the universal source of all things. (147)

Vivekananda's religion comprises *Karma, Bhakti, Jnana* and mysticism. Everyone, irrespective of religion and *Varna*, can choose one that best suits him and practise it. Yoga means union of man with God and the means to attain it. Romain Rolland defines it: "The real Vedantic yogas . . . are spiritual discipline, such as our Western philosophers have sought for in their 'Discourse of Method,' for the purpose of travelling along the straight way leading to truth. And this straight way, as in the West, is the way of experiment and reason." (187)

Yoga, as described by Swamiji, was further complemented by Aurobindo Ghose. He added Tantric Yoga to the fold of Yogas and thus carried Swamiji's synthesis of the diverse forces of life to its culmination.

Of the 'four Gospels,' *Karma-Yoga* appears to Romain Rolland the most loving. However, the relevance of Yogas varies from person to person. Vivekananda categorically explains Yogas: "To become harmoniously balanced in all these four directions is *my* ideal of religion. And this religion is attained by what we, in India, call Yoga-union. To the worker, it is union between man and the whole of humanity; to the mystic, between his Lower and Higher self; to the lover, union between himself and the God of Love and to the philosopher it is the union of *all* existence. This is what is meant by Yoga." (*Works*, 2: 388)

Karma-Yoga envisages an ethical treaty for all those who are born to lead a life of activity visible or tangible. The way of life can be either negative or positive. A mystic's way can be regarded as negative in the sense that he gainsays the world of senses. It is easy to say but is a Gordian knot to cut.

> This world's wheel within wheel is a terrible mechanism: if we put our hands in it, as soon as we are caught we are gone. . . . There are only two ways out of it; one is to give up all concern with the machine, to let it go and stand aside. . . . That is very easy to say, but is almost impossible to do. (*Works*, 1: 115)

Vivekananda here has in mind the majority of the people who are neither philosophers nor mystics nor ecstatic fellows but are mundane people. Does that mean that the working people cannot transcend this finite world? Certainly not. Does it not appeal to our conscience when he assures us the same end? "Everyone must work in the universe. . . . A current rushing down of its own nature falls into a hollow and makes a whirlpool, and, after running a little in that whirlpool, it emerges again in the form of the free current to go on unchecked. Each human life is like that current. It gets into the whirl, gets involved in the world of space, time and causation, whirls round a little, . . . and at last emerges out of it and regains its original freedom. The whole universe is doing that. . . . We are all working to get out of the dream of the world." (*Works*, 1: 98-99) And he is confident that "Through proper work done inside, it is possible to come out."

The majority of people are working day and night stretching their hands to attain perfection. In the practical life we see that the more we work the more we get attached, the more we get attached, the more miserable and lachrymose we are. Swamiji finds an answer in the *Gita*: "The ignorant work by attachment to the act; the wise man also works but beyond all attachment and solely for the good of the world. . . . Referring all action to Me, let the spirit, withdrawn into itself and free from all hope and interested motives." (Qtd. Rolland, 194) The same idea is echoed in the Christian mysticism: "Do not strive . . . either for some useful end, or temporal profit, or for hell, or for paradise, or for Grace, or to become the beloved of God . . . but purely and simply to the glory of God." (194)

The *summum bonum* of Karma-Yoga is that we ought to work incessantly for work sake without being attached to it, without desiring for anything, for desire is that root of all misery as Lord Buddha had said. We do not have any hold on the fruit—it can be both good and evil. We can only work. Attached work is a slave work. And Karma-Yoga teaches us that we should work like a master and not as a slave. It teaches us that we must be grateful to a man who gives us opportunity to serve him. Swamiji stipulates that such 'renunciation is not conditional upon faith in any God whatsoever.' Though faith makes it easier on the lower plane, it comes from inside. Success depends much upon faith on himself. How empirical is his religion that invites us 'to plunge into the world and learn the secret of work.' Again duty or ideal is a subjective thing and "each man must learn his own ideal and try to accomplish it." This path can be called the path of the body.

Nevertheless, it would be wrong to assume that it would satisfy a hermit, a mystic living in a secluded hermitage. A hermit does not need to become a householder or a householder a mystic. Raj-Yoga is, however, the most scientific and methodical of all. It is the psycho-physiological method for the direct communion with God. It awakens the *Kundalini* and explores the infinite potential of human mind and soul. It gives us a means to observe the microcosm (internal world). Swamiji not only translates *Patanjali's Yoga Sutras* but appends to it several extracts from other systems of Indian philosophy.

Raja-Yoga is divided into eight steps: *Yama, Niyama, Asana, Pranayama, Pratyahara, Dharana, Dhyana* and *Samadhi*. The practitioner of this *Yoga* has to begin with *Yama* that means non-violence, truth, honesty, chastity, non-receiving of any gift. Each one is sufficient to make one chaste and serene in thoughts and words. The first step seems to be a herculean task to achieve. When one achieves sainthood, one has to undertake physical and mental exercises and ultimately to find a posture in which one can remain for long. It keeps the Yogi fit and healthy; and gives a long life. It is to some extent akin to *Hatha-Yoga*. When one learns to have a firm erect seat, one has to perform *Pranayama* or psychic control to purify the nerves. It is not merely a practice of breathing in and out, but of controlling the *Prana*. But what is *Prana*? It is the *Prana*, as Indian philosophers believe, that is the *fons et origo* of all energy and force. *Akasa* is reckoned to be the cause of the whole creation and is said to be concocted by the power of *Prana*. So by getting control over this *Prana*, we get control over the cosmic soul. As a matter of fact senses or *Indryas* sway us in the external world. But in the journey inward one has to bring them under the yoke of the will; and this practice is called *Pratyahara*. Now this unique travel begins by fixing 'the mind on the lotus of the heart.' This gives rise to a multiplicity of waves and from among these waves, one emerges triumphant while the others retrogress. This process of unlearning the false identification of the thought-waves with the ego-sense involves 'a renewal of the mind' as St. Paul puts it. This, our Rishis called, the state of *Dhyana* or meditation. Swamiji dictates: "If the mind can be fixed on the centre for twelve seconds it will be a Dharana, twelve such Dharanas will be a Dhyana and twelve such Dhyanas will be a Samadhi." (192)

Though eight-fold paths of Raja-Yoga is an arduous task to follow, only a Ramakrishna can do so, yet it is certainly not 'unattainable' as Romain Rolland believes it. It is meant for Yogis and not for householders. And it is a fact that our motherland has reared not one but many such Yogis. The world knew only a handful of them. The brighter ones always remained unlettered, unsung. For they are souls who believe as Laotsey has said that one who knows speaks not and one who speaks knows not. Swamiji also admits that the known ones are of second rate. Though herculean it is, there are men all over the world who have been practising Raja-Yoga in one way or another.

One such Yogi, Shri Parmahansa Yoganandaji, who runs a Self Realization Fellowship Hermitage at California, teaches: "The soul of man has to ascend through five stages to God—mineral, plant, animal, man and superman." (63: 4)

The reversal of life force from matter to spirit is called *Pranayama*. By withdrawing the life current from externals through Kriya-Yoga, the consciousness begins inwardly to awaken its higher nature in God. In fact such attempts have been made to simplify the process and even science has joined hand in this pursuit but has done more harm than good to human mind. A Hippy movement in America came up and in the same pursuit relied on L.S.D. and such narcotics. Some take resort to hypnosis but they all weaken the human mind.

This does not mean that Swamiji was antipathetic to reason. Swamiji was no less conscious of it than any of the modern intellectuals. He was percipient to the dangers of thraldom and delinquency 'lurking in the way of the heart.' But man has to move forward through dangers, whatever path he may adopt, until he reaches the pure light of *Sat-Chit-Ananda* or *Amor Caritas* (Divine Love).

At the same time, he would ask the philosopher, the thinker and the intellectual to go ahead with their intellect in the quest of invisible, the other world. This ephemeral world is but of little significance to them. So Karma-Yoga, Raja-Yoga and Bhakti-Yoga will not help them. For them is Jnana-Yoga. Jnana-Yoga teaches them to understand the reality of the world—the mystery of cosmos and to 'know thyself.' Right from Socrates to the modern philosopher, most of them have stressed it. By knowing the true self, they come to know the divinity of man and the universality of the soul.

Bhakti-Yoga is the beloved path of the Romanticists, the path of heart instead of head, the path of intuition and inspiration instead of reason and intellect. Only a Bhakti-Yoga could be moved to tears at the sight of a fading daffodil, or would owe all his actions to "the wind that blows through me." Or would wait for the "spontaneous overflow of powerful feelings" to compose a poem. A T.S. Eliot would call them 'sentimental fools.' If feeling for others is foolishness, let everyone be a fool. Swamiji says: "Feel like Christ and you will be Christ. . . . It is feeling that is the life, the strength, the vitality, without which no amount of intellectual activity can reach God." Romain Rolland firmly believes that in 'ardour of this faith of love,' 'a European believer' is not inferior to his 'Asiatic' counterpart. It is irrelevant here to indulge in this kind of unending dispute in which he proceeds. Yoga cannot be a regional phenomenon, it is of universal dimension. A Bhakti-Yogi loves God, worships Him with all sorts of rituals and sings Him in mythology and attributes all sorts of names to Him. Bhakti-Yoga teaches us to love God for love's sake and not for the sake of anything. Swamiji asks the rationalists to 'let them have their God.' His God is love. He extols the virtue of it: "the greatest men I have seen in my life, the most wonderfully developed in spirituality have all come through the discipline of these rituals." (*Works*, 2: 393)

Bhakti-Yoga teaches us how to develop the love of a personal God to the universal God, and see Him in every created thing. Swamiji exhorts us to develop both pure reason and pure feeling and to balance the two by meditation.

The study of human temperament has always been of interest to psychologists. Among the numerous attempts that have been made in this direction, one of the most important modern discoveries is of Dr. William Cheldon's *The Varieties of Temperament*. His 'nomenclatory classification' of 'human temperament' is cerebrotonic, viscerotonic and somatotonic. 'All human beings are of mixed type' but one of them remains predominant. Taking this clue, Aldous Huxley has made a generalized identification of these with various religions in his article 'Religion and Temperament.' What we are concerned here is just to show that our Yoga satisfies each of these groups of mentality and manipulates these temperaments to their best end. We must fully agree with Gerald Heard who writes, "The needs of these types are met by the three main Yogas: Jnana-Yoga for intellectual, Bhakti for the predominantly devotional, and Raja-Yoga for those who combine in their natures the need for a balanced approach, mental, emotional and physical, to the divine." (Isherwood) Characteristics of viscerotonic, somatotonic and cerebrotonic are love, physical adventure and power, and intellect respectively.

Human beings are so varied in customs, temper and mentality that no 'popian manners' can be fit for the 'lofty effort of the Muse.' Vivekananda knows it full well and interprets to the world a religion of four paths that can contain all minds in it and still leaves ample freedom for further adoption as the future circumstances may demand.

Vivekananda, the Poet

It would be in the fitness of things to add to this book an evaluative chapter on Vivekananda the poet. To most of his readers, among whom are also his unwavering admirers who have gobbled up a large quantity of his writings and speeches with an avidity of literary cormorant, Vivekananda was only a dreamer, a visionary, a mystic, and a prose-writer. The poetic sensibility which the seer was richly endowed with is hardly, if ever, acknowledged by them. A perusal of his collected works will, however, reveal that Vivekananda was not only a profound thinker and religious writer but also a poet, though his poetic output is meagre and available in a thin volume published by Advaita Ashrama with an illuminating preface which is surprisingly anonymous. With considerable eloquence born of admiration, the author of the preface brings out some of the salient qualities of Vivekananda's spiritual creativity and of his Advaita-mystical outpourings, embedded in which are also his subtle esthetics and poetic credo:

> The wounded snake its hood unfurls,
> The flame stirred up doth blaze,
> The desert air resounds the calls
> Of heart struck lion's rage:
> The cloud puts forth its deluge strength
> When lightning cleaves its breast,
> When the soul is stirred to its inmost depth
> Great ones unfold their best! . . .
> All nature wear one angry frown
> To crush you out—still know, my soul,
> You are Divine. March on and on,
> Nor right nor left, but to the goal!

("The Song of the Free," 7)

The literary world, by far, does not recognize Vivekananda as a poet. K.R. Srinivasa Iyengar comments in his *Indian Writing in English*: "Occasionally he essayed English verse, too." (52) If the volume of a work is a measure of one's being a poet or not, he is certainly not so, for he wrote only thirty five poems including one in Hindi, two in Sanskrit, two translations of Sanskrit poems and seven Bengali poems. But if the 'poetic value' and the 'ulterior value' of the poem are any standard in the criticism of poetry as held by I.A. Richards, he is to be recognised a poet. (56) His first-hand experience of the inner working of the soul that reflects itself in his poems is an end in itself, and hence has an 'intrinsic value.' The moral of self-liberation and the teachings of the perennial religion that is the Advaita Vedanta may well be called the 'ulterior value' of his poetry. R.C. Prasad, in an answer to the questionnaire, emphatically asserts: "One who does not recognize him as a poet does not know what a poet is." His poems are composed with reasonable metrical skill; they exhibit his mastery of poetic language and rich poetic sensibility of the poet. Sarswathi Gowrishankar in an illuminating article on "The Poet Vivekananda" records his impression in these words: "It is of some significance to our subject to note that Swamiji's earliest interests were music and poetry, religion and philosophy; no wonder also that his works, rich in philosophical content, constitute in their perfection of imagery and purity of language some of the finest literature of the day." (*Prabudha Bharata*)

We may well recall how he once remarked to Miss MacLeod: "Do you not see that I am first and foremost a poet?" Poetry to him was neither a mere literary form nor even a vehicle for the expression of his philosophy. It was, what Romain Rolland says, "a flight of faith, without which a bird becomes a mere mechanical toy."

His lyrical effusions are 'romantic' and pervaded by the poet's individuality, non-dualism, his craving for a union with the Supreme Lord. What permeates the lyrics is the poet's central theme or his Advaita Vedanta. It is only some flat patches of didacticism that seem to be bereft of the purple touches one finds in genuine poetry. Where the poet tries to bring home to the readers his thoughtful convictions, he becomes no less matter of fact than a prosaic preacher:

> Few only know the truth. The rest will hate
> And laugh at thee, great one; but pay no heed. (*Works*, 4:395)

At times he lapses into doctrine and when he does so, the euphony of the poem breaks. Another obvious limitation of his poetry is that he could not develop a definite form of poetry and tried his hand in no other genre of poetry than lyric. His songs, minus some such patches of prosiness, are all spontaneous overflow of a soul charged with genuine feelings. Vivekananda is one of those poets who remind the reader of the great Western mystics, even of the Sufies like Rumi, and others. Insofar as his essential spiritual experiences are concerned, they remind us of St. John of the Cross, Richard Rolle of Hampole, St. Catherine of Sienna and St. Francis of Assisi. Blake is another mystic whose affinity with the Swami cannot be denied. Just as in oratory, he is akin to Lancelot Andrewes, Donne, Hooker and Newman, so in poetry he reminds the reader of the romantic mystics who often voice pantheistic experiences so akin to Vivekananda's.

One marvels at the charismatic mode of the poet which transforms devotion into rich poetry. What is a tribute to 'Kali the Mother' is a tribute to nature as well. The poet ransacks nature for his imagery and communication of the full gamut of his experiences. Nature provides him with appropriate symbols and images, most of which are hard and concrete, visual and picturesque, as in "Kali, the Mother."

In many of the poet's works, we find the recurrent theme of nature imaged and symbolized as Creatrix. God to him was not only the Father immanent in the universe but also the Creatrix at play. The *Lila*-concept is not far removed from Swamiji's thought. As a matter of fact, true spirituality springs from some such convictions that creation is a sort of divine play and that God is not only *Sat* and *Chitta* but also *Ananda*. The irrational pessimism and nihilism of the atheists are born of ignorance (*avidya*), if not of blindness to what is happening all around them. If nature is free and beyond all human control, if God's sovereignty is unchallengable and subjugates every earthly creature, one should partake of

God's *Ananda* of Mother's Play. As Vivekananda writes in "Thou Blessed Dream":

> If things go ill or well
> If joy rebounding spreads the face,
> Or sea of sorrow swells—
> A play—we each have part,
> Each one to weep or laugh as may;
> Each one his dress to don
> Its scenes, alternative shine and rain. (*Works*, 8:168)

Considered in their entirety, the poems reveal a thematic design and a pattern. It is not only imagery and Advaita philosophy that impose a unity or a design upon Vivekananda's lyrics; it is also an undercurrent of the philosophy enshrined in the Bhakti Yoga that knits the mystical songs together. Listen to the clarion call of 'Eternal Love' and 'Service Free' in the poem "To the Awakened India" that embraces in itself all the principal forms of Yoga. particularly, Bhakti and Karma Yogas.

These poems can be called the outpouring of the 'spontaneous overflow of powerful feelings.' Though they were composed at different points of time, they can be read as a single whole—a body of poetry—and not as scattered poems on different subjects. Vedanta gives unity of body and spirit to his works. His poems recapitulate the gist of his whole teaching. The concept of the oneness of soul, the divinity of man, the universality of religion, the question of awakening India by deluging it with spirituality, and cosmological and metaphysical problems are communicated forcefully through symbolic images and emotive expressions.

Swamiji was a mystic and his poems are mystical. Therefore, they have to be interpreted differently. James Scott rightly writes in *The Making of Literature*: "A perfect appreciation of a poem is only possible to a reader who has adjusted his perception of life to the poet's perception." Swamiji also stressed the need of judging a person or a thing from his or its own perspective. Like T.S. Eliot, he adored the 'theory of Impersonality' and cited the *Vedas* as its best example. No one knows the authors of the *Vedas*, the oldest scriptures of religion.

Vivekananda belongs to the Romantic school of poetry insofar as inspiration, revelation, imagination, the simplicity of language and subjective experiences of divine passion are concerned. We may well cite, an example of the apocalyptic vision of 'Kali':

> The Stars are blotted out,
> The clouds are covering clouds,
> It is darkness vibrant, sonant
> In the roaring whirling wind
> Are the souls of a million lunatics
> Just loose from the prisonhouse. (*Works*, 4: 384)

The same feeling of the chaotic world is reiterated by his contemporary W.B. Yeats in his poem "Second Coming":

> Things fall apart; the centre cannot hold;
> Mere anarchy is loosed upon the world; . . .

'Kali' in Indian mythology stands for the annihilation of the world. When the earth was filled with *Asuras* (demons), gods prayed for *Adi Shakti* to come and salvage the earth. Then the incarnation of *Shakti* took place in the form of *Kali* who took to ceaseless rampage until Shankara dramatically intervened. So Swamiji, vexed with the devilish absurdities in the world, prayed for the same *Kali* to come and destroy the world. The poem has several layers of meaning. At a deeper level, it suggests the destruction of the world of *Maya*: 'Destroys a world for e'er' for the real world is imperishable. A sannyasin would naturally seek the end of the *Maya*, the unreal self, for then only can he have the vision of 'Mother.' Another plausible explanation is that the poet appeals for the celebration of death, for he wants to infuse indomitable strength in the people. All merciful, kind and loving God has always been liked by the people. The image of 'all destroyer' God is rare in mythology and the worship of such an image is rarer still.

The celebration of death that one finds in it is not new to English poetry. We may well recall how the same craving for death is solemnly expressed in *The Bible*:

> O death, where is thy sting?
> O grave, where is thy victory? (Revelation 6:8)

Or in Walt Whitman whose poetry is pervaded by a deep consciousness of death:

> Come sweet death: be persuaded
> O beautiful death,
> In mercy come quickly. (246)

It is interesting to note that Swamiji had read Walt Whitman's poetry, particularly his *Leaves of Grass,* and his poetry echoes Whitman's in the continuity of life-cycle even beyond death. There are certain points of affinity between the two. Both can be called the poets of continuity and eternal progress. For both of them, as for any Vedantic, death is not the end of life but a chain in the life cycle. This concept has been echoed over and over again by the poets of all ages.

This visionary poem reveals Vivekananda as a poet of imagination who takes down what is dictated to him by the 'Authors of Eternity.' In the preface to his *Poems* it is written that "Kali the Mother" was written or forced itself into writing, when, during the days of pilgrimage to Kshir Bhavani (Kashmir), "the Swami was in such a high spiritual state that it seemed indeed as if his physical frame could not bear it for long." The preface quotes Sister Nivedita who accompanied him on that pilgrimage: "His brain was teeming with thoughts, he said one day, and his fingers would not rest till they were written down. Writing in a fever of inspiration, he had fallen on the floor, when he had finished—as we learnt afterwards—exhausted with his own intensity."

The intricate metrical structure of the poem also echoes it. First two lines are Iambic trimetre, third line is trochaic tetrametre; fourth line is trochaic tetrameter catelectic, fifth line is in pentametre. However, there is dominance of trimetre. There is no clear stanzaic division as we find in his other poems. All this and cluster of images 'stars,' 'clouds,' 'darkness,' 'wind,' 'lunatics,' 'prison-house,' 'Wrenching trees,' 'sea,' mountain-waves,' 'pitchy sky,' 'light' etc. and bold invocation 'Come, Mother, come!' are employed in a way to bring alive the catastrophic picture of the doom and to sound the death-knell of the world, the self into the ears of readers. 'Come, Mother come!' has the phonological effect of "Break break break" by Alfred Tennyson.

The same effect is reinforced by the use of onomatopoeic sound 'd.' The use of capital letter in words—'Death,' 'Mother,' 'Terror,' 'Thy,' 'Time,' 'All-Destroyer' (all are synonyms) and 'Dance in Destruction'—'tend to appear in truth doctrines is evidence of interest.' This heavy artillery more than a mode of emphasis is a means to impress upon the reader that he would do better to dance with joy even in death. Srinivasa Iyengar compares it with the Tamil poet Subramania Bharati's 'Oozhik Koothu' in its invocation to 'the destroyer of the worlds.' But Swamiji in his lecture "The Vedanta in All its Phases" compares this particular line—"The clouds are covering clouds" with one 'Darkness which can be penetrated with the point of a needle' from Kalidasa and with 'No light but rather darkness visible' from Milton. The preponderance of the dark side of nature in the *Samhitas* is attributed to the tropical climate of the land. But these are not the most sublime portion of the *Samhitas*. The obvious limitation is its attempt to find solution in the external world. Swamiji says in "Vedanta and Indian Life":

> Take for instance, Milton, Dante, Homer or any of the Western poets. There are wonderfully sublime passages in them; but there it is always a grasping at infinity through the senses, the muscles, . . . We find the same attempts made in the *Samhita* portion. . . . But they found out very soon that the Infinite cannot be reached in that way . . . and so they fell back upon other explanations. The language became new in the *Upanishads*; it is almost negative, it is sometimes, chaotic, sometimes taking you beyond the senses. (*Works*, 3:234-35)

The use of negative language in some of his poems can safely be attributed to the language of the *Upanishads*. Another example of this kind of poem is "The Hymn of Creation" that is the translation of the tenth *Mandal* of the *Rig-Veda*.

> Existence was not then, nor non-existence.

> The world was not, the sky beyond was neither.
> (*Works*, 6:178)

The same native language is employed in some of his Bengali poems like "The Hymn of Samadhi," "The Dance of Shiva," "And Let Shyama Dance There." But this negative language is employed for the world of Maya, for our senses cannot know the microcosm. Therefore our Rishi said "*Neti, Neti*" "not this not this." Reality is not negated but the perverted picture of Reality that appears in the realm of Maya is refuted. For we know that he can also speak in the most sublime and in the boldest Vedantic term—'*Aham Brahma Asmi.*' See, for example, "The Song of the Free":

> From dreams awake from bonds be free!
> Be not afraid. This mystery,
> My shadow, cannot frighten me!
> Know once for all that I am He! (*Poems*, 7)

The same Advaitic concept of *Brahma* is taught in the "Song of the Sannyasin." It is a kind of prayer consciously composed for daily practice at his *Asrama*. The poem contains in itself the gist of his whole teachings expressed in beautiful language. It is remarkable for its appeal to the Sannyasin to be free from all bonds, to conquer all by conquering the self, to know thyself—know that you are *Atman*, 'the sexless self,' and for the universality and the oneness of the soul—'there is but One—The Free—The Knower—Self,' for his exhortation for renunciation, 'do I renounce, All heavens and earths and hells, all hope and fears,' for its ethical value 'Truth never comes where lust and frame and greed of gain reside' prescribed for a Sannyasin, for his emphasis is on the quest for Truth, for the spiritual realization and for its cosmological union of man with the Universe, "The 'I' Has All become, the All is 'I'."

"It is this insight—this vision of the unseen Reality," says Suniti Kumar Chatterji, "that makes poetry or any other kind of literature have a supreme value." Chatterji echoes what Goethe, Plato, Aristotle and Romantic poets like Blake, Coleridge, Wordsworth and Shelley have cherished—a deep penetrating insight into things—visible and invisible.

Though Vivekananda's poems are primarily addressed to some one or written for a particular occasion, they have a universal appeal, transcending the barriers of time and place. His ideas of Advaita and of chastity and charity have been woven through centuries of general and personal experience in a changing pattern. The very number of cultures, religions and languages and of associations with the experiences of other poets and mystics is enough to suggest its universality. For example, the moral of "The Song of the Sannyasin" is true to all seekers of God in all ages. "Hold on Yet a While, Brave Heart" was written to the Maharaja of Khetri, but still works as a source of inspiration for all those who are the victims of this world of senses. "To the Awakened India" was written in the context of pre-independent India to awaken the masses but is still relevant to our age. How can the message to be 'strong and steady,' 'Blissful, bold, and free' or of 'infinite love' lose its relevance? Has not his appeal for the liberation of all colonies in "To the Fourth of July" kept them inspiring? Or will ever the poetic value of this celebration of the anniversary of the American Declaration of Independence cease? Similarly "The Living God" was written to an American friend, "A Benediction" to Sister Nivedita, "Requiescat in Pace" on J.J. Goodwin's death; "My Play is Done" was written about himself. But they all are steeped in Vedantic colour and hence appeal to our soul and intellect.

Vedantic as they are, they owe a great deal to his readings of the *Vedas*, the *Upanishads*, the *Ramayana*, the *Mahabharata*, the *Gita*, the *Imitation of Christ*, the *Light of Asia*, works of Kalidasa and other Sanskrit and Bengali works. He found the divinities of love, of motherland, of beauty and chastity in Greek literature. He had an indirect but close contact with this literature through English and Latin. Chaucer, Milton, Keats, Shelley, Browning and Tennyson wafted into his soul the fragrant breeze of the Greek lyric poets along with the transcendental beauty as well as the cosmic aspect of the Greek myths. He had also studied Greek history and mythology. Through William Jones, the Vedantic influence got into the west and reflected itself in the Romantic and the Victorian poetry. Confronted with the ideas of perennial religion in the poetry of Wordsworth, Coleridge, Shelley and Whitman, his conviction got reinforced. The transcendental state of mind is well depicted in Wordsworth's *Tintern Abbey.* Later on Shri Ramakrishna gave a practical demonstration of it. Even when he consoles a grieved heart, he adopts Shelley's line "If winter comes can spring be far behind" in this way:

> No Winter was but summer came behind,
> Each hollow crests the wave,
> They push each other in light and shade;
> Be steady then and brave. (*Works*, 4:390)

Both Wordsworth and Swamiji invest some sort of mystic radiance in an infant. Wordsworth in *The Prelude* writes:

> Blest the infant Babe, . . .
> Nursed in his Mother's arms, who sinks to sleep
> Rocked on his Mother's breast; who with his soul
> Drinks in the feelings of his Mother's eye!

A few lines from Swamiji's "Who Knows How Mother Plays!"

> Perchance the child had glimpse
> Of shades, behind the scenes,
> With eager eyes and strained, . . .
> Who knows but Mother, how,
> And where, and when, they come? (*Works*, 5: 439)

In Wordsworth there is a filial bond of Nature that links the child with the world. In Vivekananda, it is the Mother's play. Wordsworth excels in the poetic beauty and in the richness of images that depict the development of a child photographically. Again, they come close to each other in the depiction of transcendental state of mind. Vivekananda in "The Song of the Free" presents the same picture that he finds in Wordsworth's "Excursion" that was taught to him at his college by Professor Hastie. Both these poems present the realization of God as an Impersonal Being:

> I am Beyond all sense, all thought,

The witness of the Universe.
Not two nor many this but one.
And thus in me all ones I have,
I cannot hate, I cannot shun
Myself from me—I can but love.
From dreams awake, from bonds be free.
Be not afraid, This mystery
My shadow cannot frighten me.
Know once for all that I am He. (*Poems*, 8)

Again his exhortation to march forward in the "Awakened India" echoes Lord Tennyson's "The Charge of the Light Brigade."

References are not so wide to puzzle a Hindu reader who is supposed to be conversant with his mythology and scriptures. The familiar references to 'Himalaya's daughter Uma,' 'Mother Kali,' Shiva, Shyam, Ganga, Sita, Ram give a serenity to the atmosphere, and they touch our conscience. We can easily detect the influence of the Vendanta. The recurrent use of 'Om Tat Sat Om,' Maya, Atman, attributes to God—'He free, the knower-self' (*Satchittananda*), 'Awake, arise and dream no more'—an adaptation of *Utisthit jagratvaranya bodhat*'. 'I am he!' the translation of *So-aham*, and many more phrases are enough to suggest the Vedantic influence on his poetry. "The Song of the Sannyasin" is full of quotations and allusions derived from the *Gita*. Again the concept of *Tatvamasi* repeatedly appears in his poems. This term appears in stanza five, six, seven, and eight in different ways in the poem "To the Awakened India"—'One in all,' 'but one,' 'Truth alone' and 'Be one with it.' So from the statement of fact, he moves to the realization of the fact. We have also Biblical images like 'deluge,' 'heaven' etc. in his poems.

Vivekananda broke away from the poetic trends of 'Derozio men' and experimented, though unconsciously, with a new kind of his own in lyric form. His spiritual and mystic creativity led to the development of *Mantric* poetry, which was later perfected by Aurobindo. He brought poetry close to the Vedic *Mantra*. It was natural for him to opt for the medium of the Vedic *Mantra* though he was conversant with the poetic trends in English literature. He translated a portion of Mandal X of the *Rig-Veda* in the poem entitled "The Hymn of Creation." Akhauri Rajendra Prasad in his article "The Poetical Corpus of Vivekananda" compares it with *Savitri*: "The opening lines of 'The Hymn of Creation' . . . in majesty and poetic beauty remind us of the opening lines of Sri Aurobindo's *Savitri* with the only difference that what Sri Aurobindo achieves with labour and strain is effortlessly and spontaneously achieved by Vivekananda." (Sinha, 81) However, there is a great difference between the two. "The Hymn of Creation" draws its 'majesty' from the *Rig-Veda*. Aurobindo's *Savitri* is the product of his own poetic genius. It is at par with the epics of Milton. What the Swami initiated in English poetry, Aurobindo brought it to fruition. As V.K. Gokak writes, Vivekananda "wrote philosophic and mystic lyric poetry in English and laid the foundation of a new tradition in Indian literature even before Tagore's *Gitanjali* was known to the Indian people in English."

The pantheism of Vivekananda is more sublimated than that of Shelley. Shelley could not develop any systematic philosophy. Vivekananda says that when a man realizes the all-pervadingness of God through any of the four paths—*Raja, Karma, Bhakti* or *Jnana-Yoga*, he sees 'the One in All' 'The Mother that resides in all as Power and Life.' Vivekananda's affinity with the Sufi mystic Baba Kuhi of Shiraz can be illustrated with this verse:

> In all the eye discovered—only God I saw.
> Like a candle I was melting in His fire:
> Amidst the flames outflanking—only God I saw.
> Myself with mine eyes I saw most clearly,
> But when I looked with God's eyes—only God I saw.
> I passed away into nothingness, I vanished,
> And lo, I was the all-living—only God I saw. (Qtd. Sen, 151)

Furthermore, the way he wishes natural objects 'cloud-belted Snows,' 'The heavenly River' and 'Deodar shades' to help man realize his goal—'Strength' and 'eternal peace'—reminds one of Shelley's invocation to the 'West Wind' though for a different purpose. He is a pantheist like Shelley but he cannot be called aeolian. In his attempt for mystic union with God, he comes closer to Coleridge than to Shelley. These lines from Coleridge's "Ode to Dejection" are identical with Vivekananda's:

> The Passion & the Life whose Fountains are within!
> These lifeless Shapes, around, below, above,
> O what can they impart?
> When even the gentle Thought, that thou, my Love!
> Art gazing now, like me, . . .

Though a sense of loss and confirmation of the mystical relationship with nature runs through Coleridge's poetry, there is a great difference between the two. In Wordsworth and De La Mare, we have the quest for 'Truth' and 'Reality.' So they could not speak with authority. Vivekananda was a mystic, they were not. He first realized the 'Truth' and then expressed his experiences in prose and poetry with authority, profundity and subtlety. Take for example a few stanzas from "The Song of the Free":

> Know these are but the outer crust
> All space and time, all effect, cause,
> I am beyond all sense, all thought,
> The witness of the Universe!
> Not two nor many this but one.
> And thus in me all ones I have,
> I cannot hate, I cannot shun
> Myself from me—I can but love!
> From dreams awake, from bonds be free!
> Be not afraid. This mystery,
> My Shadow, cannot frighten me!
> Know once for all that I am He! (*Poems*, 7)

Only a Vivekananda can speak like this. His poems represent the various facets of his personality. We have seen how "The Song of the Sannyasin" and "The Song of the Free" represent him as an Advaitin, in some other poems like "Kali The Mother," "Who Knows, How Mother Plays," "Angels Unawares," "My play Is Done," "A Hymn of Surrender to Sri Ramakrishna" (in Sanskrit) and "A Hymn to the Divinities of Sri Ramakrishna," spoke in dualistic terms. This echoes his love and veneration shown for it in his lectures.

But strikingly different is the tone in the poem "The Living God" that shows his romanticism in the sense that it breaks 'all other idols!' In this sense it shows the iconoclastic facet of his temperament that burst out in the moment of deep agony. Normally he was not an idol breaker. In this poem as elsewhere, he shows his preference for the worship of 'the living God'—the poor, the weak, the down-trodden, the wretch. He gave a clarion call for 'Eternal Love and Service Free.'

> Ye fools! who neglect the living God,
> And His infinite reflections with which the world is full.
> While ye run after imaginary shadows,
> That lead alone to fights and quarrels,
> Him worship, the only visible!
> Break all other idols! (*Works*, 8:169)

This was a direct attack on the dualistic trend in religions and a favour for the Advaitic concept of God:

> He who is in you and outside you,
> Who works through all hands,
> Who walks on all feet,
> Whose body are all ye,
> Him worship . . . (*Works*, 8:169)

The slow rhythmic movement coupled with the use of imperatives make it a saintly and didactic piece.

There is complete identification of his personality with the poverty, sufferings and sorrows of his countrymen, nay of the whole world. He could partake of the griefs of millions because he was himself one with them:

> Not two nor many, 'tis but one.

It is said that the poet cannot escape the effect of his times and the milieu, however escapist he may be. In the literal sense of the term, he may be called an escapist for he wants to escape the agonies of life by transcending the physical world and by delving deep into the other world—the world of spirit. His poems do not deal with the absurdities in the society, the maladies of the British yoke or the national movement. Though he was not involved in the political movement, he awakened India from its long stupor by deluging it with spirituality. His poem "Awakened India" shows beyond doubt how much nationalist he was, how much alive to the situation he was.

> Once more awake!
> For sleep it was, not death, to bring thee life
> Anew and rest to lotus-eyes for visions
> Daring yet. The world in need awaits, O Truth!
> No death for thee!
> Resume thy march,
> With gentle feet that would not break the
> Peaceful rest even of the roadside dust
> That lies so low. Yet strong and steady,
> Blissful, bold, and free. Awakener, ever
> Forward! speak thy stirring words.
> Thy home is gone,
> Where loving hearts had brought thee up and
> Watched with joy thy growth. But Fate is strong—
> This is the Law—all things come back to the source
> They sprung, their strength to renew. (*Works*, 4:387)

Vivekananda wanted to rejuvenate Indians by inducing a sense of pride in them and by showing how they were equal to other races. He does not talk of India's freedom but the freedom of all nations in his poem "To the Fourth of July" that celebrates the anniversary of America's freedom. He believes that the freedom of the nation will come through individual freedom. "To the Fourth of July" is also an invocation to the Sun-God: 'Move on, O Lord, in thy restless path,' and echoes the invocation contained in *Gayatri Mantra—Om bhur bhuva Svaha tatsaviturwarenyam bhargo devasya dhimahi dhiyo yo na Prachodyat*! It is both *Mantra* and prayer rolled into one to lead, not only the person offering prayers, but also mankind as a whole, from darkness to light.

Vivekananda's being a moral teacher is established by his poems as well. Take for example "Hold on Yet a While, Brave Heart" in which he tells the Maharaja of Khetri not to lose heart even when stars are in rough weather and keep on working. The poem gives a great moral teaching to everyone that God helps one who helps oneself.

Vivekananda's deep love and compassion for his disciples explicitly comes out in his short poem "Benediction" addressed to Sister Nivedita.

Above all, his only autobiographical poem 'My Play is Done' that throws light on his personal life, seems to be one of the supreme creations of his poetic genius. The poet seems to be physically exhausted as he has "almost exhausted himself by the uninterrupted work of class and public lecturing": "I am sick of this unending force."

This is the reaction of a Sannyasin against the public fame and name hurled on him. There are many other such lines in the poem that point to the seminal influence of a sensitive youth "ever rising, ever falling with the waves of time." In a meditative sequence of reflections on the enigma of time, Vivekananda recalls the experiences of his struggling life:

> From fleeting scene to scene ephemeral,
> With life's currents' ebb and flow. (*Works*, 6:175)

> You sent me out in the dark to play,
> and wore a frightful mask;
> Then hope departed, terror came,
> and play became a task.
> Tossed to and fro, from wave to wave
> in this seething, surging seas. (*Works*, 6:176)

The latter is reminiscent of his early life. The poem is a reflection on the pensive mood of the poet—the suffering of long hours of pitiless self questioning, personal sorrow in the death of his father, the sudden plunge into acute poverty and the heart breaking attempt to secure livelihood. Moving from his birth "You sent me out" to the demise of his Guru "Then hope departed," to the task of leading his disciples and fulfilling his desire for 'wanderzahare,' 'Tossed to and fro,' the poem ends with his deepest fascination for *nirvikalpa samadhi*:

> Let never more delusive dreams
> veil off thy face from me.
> My play is done, O Mother,
> break my chains and make me free! (*Works*, 6:177)

We may well recall, in this context how Shri Ramakrishna, having made him go into Samadhi once and taking away the key to it told him that this key would remain with him until he accomplished the work assigned to him by Mother *Kali*. And in 1895 he says to Mother that 'My play is done' and so he must be allowed to plunge into *nirvikalpa samadhi*. But perhaps his play was not done and so his appeal remained pending until 1902 when he entered into *nirvikalpa samadhi*.

The poem is not only an autobiographical recollection of his private experiences but also a philosophical discourse on subjects like 'life' and 'death':

> Where life is living death, alas! and death—
> who knows but 'tis
> Another Start, another round of his old wheel
> of grief and bliss? (*Works*, 6:176)

What strikes one is the reflective nature of the poem and the fulfilment of the standard of a good poem laid down by T.S. Eliot who says that in a good poem the personal and private agonies and pleasures are transmuted into something impersonal and universal:

> Where children dream bright, golden dreams,
> too soon to find them dust,
> And aye look back to hope long lost
> and life a mass of rust! (*Works*, 6:176)

The optimism and brightness of a child and the feeling of pessimism in old age are themes common enough in English poetry. The poet seems to be fully convinced of the futility of this ephemeral world and of what Lord Buddha had said that desire was the cause of all misery. Here Vivekananda says the same thing in a symbolic language in which hope or desire is represented by 'motor' and the natural concomitant of it—'grief' and 'joy' are represented by its 'pokes.' Like a romantic, he wants to escape this world and go beyond it where there is neither sorrow nor joy. The same spirit is conveyed in his letter LX to Mrs. Bull (Feb. 1895).

A phonological consideration reveals ubiquitous alliteration of 'ing' inflection that gives, besides a singsong rhythm and verbal musicality, an effect of his ceaseless bubbling life of activity; and shows a conviction for the continuity of life-line even after death, for death is nothing but a chain in the life cycle. The poet, however, wants to escape from the cycle of birth and death into *Nirvan* that promises a new timeless condition which is not subject to intellectual or linguistic qualification.

The poem "The Cup" also conveys 'a sense of heroism and martyrdom.' V.K. Gokak gives a brief but illuminating account of the poem: "Swami Vivekananda's poem 'The Cup' gives us all the aroma of Indian Renaissance, its tone of pain and suffering, its fortitude, and sense of disciplined and stoic calm, its sense of heroism and even martyrdom but also the serene note of victory sounding through sorrow and the joy that is promised at the end. It is a remarkable poem, full of the flavour of the spoken language, but for a few words like 'drear' and 'bid.' Vivekananda had apparently appreciated the beauty of English spoken during his visit to the states and it figures in this poem, in all its freshness. What is more, the poem gives a glimpse of Vivekananda's life as he saw it":

> This is your road—a painful road and drear.
> I made the stones that never give you rest.
> I set your friends in pleasant ways and clear,
> And he shall come like you, unto My breast.
> But you, My child, must travel here. (*Works*, 6:177)

Swamiji achieves a symphony of apparently contradictory conditions: hope and despair, life and death, faith and reason and ideal and practical.

> I look behind and after
> And find that all is right,
> In my deepest sorrow
> There is a soul of light. (*Works*, 8:168)

What appears contradictory to common man is to the poet a reality in relation to something. He does not negate Maya as Buddha did but accepted it as a reality. Despite all despair and frustration that he realizes in life he comes close to Ulysses in Homer's *Odyssey* who is full of hope of reaching his destination.

His poems are largely unrhymed save a few—"To an Early Violet," "The Cup," "A Benediction" and "An Interesting Correspondence." But the movement of the verse is not harsh; rather there is a smooth gliding movement of the verse. The musical effect is achieved through alliteration, assonance and consonance:

> Speed forth, O Soul! upon thy star-strewn path (*Works*, 4:389)
> That lies so low Yet strong and steady (*Works*, 4:387)
> Let darkness go; the will-o'-the-wisp that leads
> With blinking light to pile more gloom on gloom.
> (*Works*, 4:393)

Or through internal rhyming;

> Let go thy hold, Sannyasin bold! (*Works*, 4:394)
> Ever rising, ever falling with the waves of time,
> still rolling on I go
> From fleeting scene to scene ephemeral (*Works*, 6:175)

The pervasive use of present participle in poems like "My Play is Done" and the above mentioned poetic devices not only give a cadence to the verse but also reinforce the meaning and add a colour to it. Coupled with proper use of diction and varied range of images, they provide structural unity and cohesiveness to the poem. They also indicate how much conscious of the beauty and efficacy of the poem Vivekananda was. Vivekananda does not seem to be very particular about a uniform metre. Feet keeps on changing in a poem. And his poems are more or less formless save a few. However, there are a few poems like "Requiescat in Pace" and "The Song of the Sannyasin," in iambic and trochaic pentameter or "A Benediction" in purely trochaic tetrametre or "To an Early Violet" in trochaic tetrametre followed by iambic trimetre in a successive pattern. About metrical structure, the conclusion arrived at is that his favourite metres are trimetre, tetrametre and pentametre with iambic and trochaic feet. They are often mixed in the poem.

There is yet another aspect of Vivekananda, the poet, that should not be ignored. Take out all his poems and yet he will be a poet. A perusal of his prose works reveals the poet behind the scene. In them he comes out like D.H. Lawrence, Virginia Woolf, James Joyce and Proust as a poet in prose. If poetry means stirring of soul, spring of imagination, touching the chords of heart and sensuous apprehension of experiences, Vivekananda must also be counted among the poets in prose. In the modern sense of the term, poetry is no longer confined to the rigorous format of verse. If Chekhov and Ionesco can be called poets on the stage why not Vivekananda? It is a historical fact that poetry and oratory were very close to each other. Vivekananda frequently uses poetic images in his speeches that are largely rhythmic; and they are remarkable for the poetic fire of a seer. Not to say of other writing and speeches, his work 'Memoirs of European Travel' is enough to prove it. He writes: "I owe you a description of the sea-voyage for seven days which will be full of poetry and interest and be written in a polished, rhetorical style." (*Works*, 7:298) Again he writes: "to prove that I am not wholly devoid of the poetic instinct either, I set myself to the task with God's name." (*Works*, 7:299) And he wrote in splendid poetic prose full of poetic images:

> Anyhow, getting up from bed late night I found that Mother evidently could not bear staying in that awkward vessel and was trying to force her passage out of it. I thought it most dangerous, for if Mother chose to reenact here those previous scenes of her life, such as piercing the Himalayas, washing away the great elephant Airavata, and pulling down the hut

of the sage Jahnu, then it would be a terrible affair.

(*Works*, 7:302)

A superb lyrical power of narration can be seen in his opening speech at the Parliament of Religions—"I thank you in the name of . . . I thank you in the name of . . . I thank you in the name of . . . "—that captivated the mind and heart of the "Sisters and Brothers of America" The frequent use of images in his speeches and writings is essentially the gift of a poets's imagination. Thus in this way also Vivekananda is a poet *par excellence*.

Finally we may well say that Vivekananda, the poet, employed a range of metrical and stanzaic forms, and a whole range of images from commonplace to metaphysics, from tied to free images; but there is a uniformity of tone (religious and saintly), of mood (pensive) and of the idea of oneness of soul in most of his poems. The uniformity of his ideas and morals provide one of the links between the poet and the preacher. He may be regarded as a minor Indian-English poet from the point of view of total poetic output, but he is no less rich in the poetic sensibility and in the exposition of spiritual and religious poetry than his contemporaries.

Prose Style

Swami Vivekananda's prose presents the dichotomy of style—the brevity, understatement and aphorisms of a saint, and lucid, transparent and loose style of a preacher and orator. Born and brought up in Indian culture, he wrote and spoke in English with ease and mastery of a mother tongue. Though he is repetitive in his speeches, Vivekananda maintains brevity, compactness and precision in his writings, especially his "Paper on Hinduism," "Reincarnation" and *Raja-Yoga*. In his discourses and talks, he speaks sometimes in aphorisms and sometimes through parables.

However outspoken Vivekananda may be, his language is nowhere flippant or flamboyant. He maintains the decorum of a saint. The whole personality of Swamiji is reflected in his style. Buffon's definition of style—"style it is the man himself"—stands true to his style that reflects the whole facet of Vivekananda—his mood and temperament. This, as we know, is an achievement that a writer can boast of. Though there is no trace of such pride in him. variation in style in accordance with the subject and occasion characterizes his sense of propriety. We can see how his style departs from the usual Baconian and Senecan style whenever he speaks about his master, Ramakrishna; pithy sentences voluntarily get changed into long periodical ones. It comes a bit close to Ciceronian style: "When Prof. Max Mueller, who occupies in the West the first rank in the field of Indian religion, philosophy, and literature, published with a devoted heart a short sketch of Shri Ramakrishna's life in the nineteenth century for the benefit of Europeans and Americans, it is needless to say that a bitter feeling of burning rancour made its appearance amongst those two classes of people referred to above." (*Works*, 5: 414-15) But this is not typical of his style. His writings, though they are rhetorical prose, aptly display the qualities of epigrammatism, the economy of words, a virile style, the serene, calm, placid atmosphere, stirring rhythm and lucid and transparent composition.

Vivekananda's success lies in reviving the spirit of true religion, its philosophy, its science, and reconciling the concepts of religion with those of science. His was the age when religion was considered no more than a myth. A spirit of rational inquiry and scientific reasoning was supervening upon an age of child-like faith. He discarded the dogmas of religion and gave a scientific interpretation to it so that it may stand true to the test of science. He expressed this desire in one of his letters to a disciple: "The dry, abstract Advaita must become living—poetic—in every day life; out of hopelessly intricate mythology must come concrete moral forms; and out of bewildering Yogi-ism must come the most scientific and practical psychology—and all this must be put in a form so that a child may grasp it. That is my life's work." (*Works*, 5: 104-5, Ep. LVIII) The letter indirectly throws light on his style. It is clear that he wanted to hammer out like Swift a simple, serviceable style bare of ornament. The second point in the letter is that the style should be made concrete as far as possible. And this, one finds, particularly in his case who wrote or spoke on mainly abstract subjects, an arduous task if not impossible. However hard one may try, one cannot do away with abstract terminology and phraseology like Maya, soul, prana, Bhakti, intuition, love, etc, in a discussion of abstract philosophy. Swamiji, by way of giving concrete examples and illustrations, achieves to a reasonable extent the concreteness of style that can be called a great achievement of his prose style. A superb example of it can be found in his illustration of the concept of Maya:

> Then, there is the tremendous fact of death. The whole world is going towards death; everything dies. All our progress, our vanities, our reforms, our luxuries, our wealth, our knowledge, have that one end—death. That is all that is certain. Cities come and go, empires rise and fall, planets break into pieces and crumble into dust, to be blown about by the atmospheres of other planets. Thus it has been going on from

> time without beginning. Death is the end of everything. Death is the end of life, of beauty, of wealth, of power, of virtue too. Saints die and sinners die, kings die and beggars die. They are all going to death, and yet this tremendous clinging on to life exists. Somehow, we do not know why we cling to life; we cannot give it up. And this is Maya.
>
> The mother is nursing a child with great care; all her soul, her life, is in that child. The child grows, becomes a man, and perchance becomes a blackguard and a brute, kicks her and beats her everyday; and yet the mother clings to the child; and when her reason awakes, she covers it up with the idea of love. She little thinks that it is not love, that it is something which has got hold of her nerves, which she cannot shake off; however she may try, she cannot shake off the bondage she is in. And this is Maya. (*Works*, 2: 92-93)

If Vivekananda's writings have been kept so much alive for their theme or subject, they are no less because of his style—simple, virile and modern. Had they been in scholarly language, they would have died out before long the way many other scholarly writings on Vedic subjects have. Vivekananda's works, on the other hand, have been translated into several languages and are read the world over. It is rightly written in the *Introduction* to his *Complete Works*: "For ages to come the Hindu man who would verify, the Hindu mother who would teach her children, what was the faith of their ancestors will turn to the pages of these books for assurance and light. Long after the language has disappeared from India, the gift that has here been made through that language, to the world, will remain and bear its fruit in East and West alike." (*Works*, 1: ix)

His prose work is so rich and varied in subject that it encompasses in itself almost all the major forms of style, ranging from narrative to epistolary, from subjective to objective and from formal to informal. Two broad categories of his prose-works can be made—oratorical prose and written prose. Except his letters, "His Paper on Hinduism" and some other pieces, his prose is oratorical and hence its language is quite colloquial. But the elements of written and spoken are indivisibly mixed. Surprisingly enough, he spoke without any notes; and yet not a single paragraph has a disjointed look. Each sentence and each paragraph is linked with the preceding one syntactically and thematically. Though there are repetitions, Vivekananda maintains the precision and compactness of written English:

> I know the difficulties. Tremendous they are, and ninety percent of us become discouraged and lose heart, and in our turn, often become pessimists and cease to believe in sincerity, love, and all that is grand and noble. So we find men who in the freshness of their lives have been forgiving, kind, simple, and guileless, become in old age lying masks of men. Their minds are a mass of intricacy. . . . There is death in the heart, for cold hands have seized upon it, and it can no more act, even to utter a curse, even to use a harsh word.
>
> All this we have to avoid, therefore I say, we require super divine power. (*Works*. 2: 6)

We can see how skilfully each sentence is linked with another and the second paragraph is linked with the first one by the linker 'all this.' The second sentence is linked with the first one with the pronoun 'they' of the object 'difficulties.' There is an unhindered flow of ideas. Sentences like 'They don't curse, not become angry,' or 'they cannot' are examples of spoken English. But the passage has the compactness and precision of genuine subjective prose. One, however, marvels at the word 'super divine' and wonders what can be the state above Godhood.

As far as the power of orderly arrangement of ideas is concerned, it is not judged from one or two passages, but emerges from the whole context. "The Powers of the Mind," "Hints on Practical Spirituality," his lecture "My Plan of Campaign" and other lectures from Colombo to Almora group are imbued with the subjectivity of style that one finds in the prose of Hazlitt and Charles Lamb. In this group of writings, the writer comes out vividly with his likes and dislikes, his personal impressions on the subject of discussion. Even when the subject is objective like Vedanta, Maya, science, power of mind, etc., he gives a personal touch to it. While talking about practical Vedanta in his lecture delivered in London, he gives a subjective interpretation of it, though in the light of Hindu scriptures. He begins:

> I have been asked to say something about the practical position of the Vedanta philosophy. As I have told you, theory is very good indeed, but how are we to carry it into practice? If it be absolutely impracticable, no theory is of any value whatever, except as intellectual gymnastics. (*Works*, 2: 291)

He gives a subjective analysis of such a subject as theory of heredity and theory of evolution but nowhere is he whimsical—he proceeds along the line of ratiocination and inductive method of Bacon. Like classical preachers and orators, he is adroit in inventing ingenious analogies:

> A man plays a tune on a piano, he places each finger on each key consciously. He repeats this process till the movement of the fingers becomes a habit. He then plays a tune without having to pay special attention to each particular key. Similarly, we find in regard to ourselves that our tendencies are the result of past conscious action. (*Works*, 2: 320)

His prose has his authorial presence or voice that he projects in order to achieve the emotional responses of the reader and the audience. This personal mark on his prose is born of his direct experience of truth. His 'words come out from the depth of truth,' to use Derozio's phrase. He dives into the "depths of time" and brings out the whole body of sublimity that one rarely finds elsewhere. Unlike Derozio who articulates his Weltschmerz "which human eye may never more behold," Swamiji is full of optimism and predicts the fall of colonialism and the dawn of *Satyuga*.

In the West, he rarely spoke on a subjective theme. One of such speeches is "My Life and Mission" delivered on 27th January 1900. Beginning with a historical background of India in a pictorial language, he moves on to present his own life. "I would have to go from house to house to collect sufficient for one meal. And then the bread was so hard, it made my mouth bleed to eat it. . . . Then I would put it in a pot and pour over it water" (*Works*, 8: 84) Then he narrates the life of his Guru—how he had grown up into a monk and how he was devoid of body consciousness: "He never knew whether he was living or dying or anything. Sometimes, when talking, he would get so excited that if he sat on live charcoals; he did not know it. Live Charcoals!" (*Works*, 8: 82) In this speech, Vivekananda carried the audience to a world of India in imagination.

The language and style is colloquial and natural but expressive. Vivekananda's speeches are full of rhetorical qualities that have already been delineated in the chapter "Swamiji—The Orator." Style has its origin in the school of rhetoric. Aristotle, Longinus, Cicero and Quintillion were the masters of rhetoric and study of their works gave Swamiji a sense of organic style and a sense of decorum. In rhetoric, he employed the whole range of stylistic armoury that a Gladstone would have employed to achieve the desired end.

Vivekananda's letters are the best example of his personal, private and subjective prose as they throw light on his private life—his diffidence. his early craving for name, his iconoclasm, his feelings for the priest in India, the 'heathen Indian' and his cynicism. Here is an excerpt from his letters: "Kick out the priests who are always against progress, because they would never mend, their hearts would never become big. They are the offspring of centuries of superstition and tyranny. Root out priestcraft first." (*Works*, 5: 10, Ep. III)

One does not find Vivekananda speaking so in the public. He warned Alasinga, to whom this letter was written, not to publish it—"calm and silent and steady work, and no newspaper humbug." Does it not show the diffidence in him? At times he grows bitter in tone in his letter: "Do not go about begging from the Hindu beggars." (*Works*, 5: 81, Ep. XXXIX) Nowhere else can one find such vituperation from his lips as in this:

> You race of cowards—physical, moral and spiritual! You animals fit to be treated as you are with two ideas before you—lust and money—you want to prod a Sannyasin to life of constant fighting. (*Works*, 5: 80, Ep. XXXIX)
>
> If anybody is born of a low caste in our country he is gone for ever. there is no hope for him. (*Works*. 5: 26. Ep. VI)

Or his desire to make himself heard: "Employ the money you have in printing and publishing this short speech; and translating it into the vernaculars, throw it broadcast; that will keep us before the national mind." (*Works*, 5: 28, Ep. VII) Or his love to read papers about himself: "Now send always Indian newspapers about me to me over here. I want to read them in the papers themselves—do you know?" (*Works*, 5: 40, Ep. XIII) This desire ceased in a year when he achieved the worldwide popularity as he wrote to Alasinga: "I am sorry you still continue to send me pamphlets and newspapers, which I have written you several times not to do. I have no time to peruse them." (*Works*, 5: 66, Ep. XXX)

But his letters are by no means merely a personal account or reportage; they at times take the shape of an article, a travelogue and a poem. His letters minus the reportage contained in them put together can be a classic in the philosophical work of art. They exhibit his deep insight into human psyche, his gradual progression and can be read as a moral treatise.

His letter (III) to Alasinga on 10th July 1893 and another on 20th Aug. 1893 can be read as travelogues in which he gives a memoir of his expedition from India to Chicago. In one of his letters to Professor John Henry Wright, he wrote a poem without a caption (Ep. IX, Vol. 7). A cardinal case in point is "An Interesting Correspondence" written in rhymed verse.

> Now Sister Mary,
> You need not be sorry
> For the hard raps I gave you,
> You know full well,
> Though you like me tell,
> With my whole heart I love you. (*Works*, 8: 162)

A perusal of his letters reveals that they are in an informal and loose style. Colloquial expressions and phrases, Sanskrit quotations and Hindi phrases (when he wrote to the Indians) and quotations from scriptures are often used. They are written in a simple and conversational language of day-to-day life. They are innocent of metaphors and other literary tropes in general. In style they depart from his oratory. None of the rhetorical devices of his oratory can be traced in his letters.

Many of his subjects demand impersonal, objective and hence formal style. When they do so, Swamiji comes up like a critic to interpret the subject like the *Gita, Raja-Yoga, Karma-Yoga, Bhakti-Yoga, Jnana-Yoga*, Practical Vedanta, Mohammed and many more objectively. He confesses that not a single idea that he teaches is his own. He is an interpreter who has elucidated the complex and abstruse philosophies, metaphysics and mythology of our classical scriptures which are in their original form incomprehensible to the common man, nay even to the elite. The credit goes to him for making accessible to the world the infinite reservoir of knowledge and wisdom contained in the Hindu scriptures. William James pays his tribute:

> To interpret absolute monism worthily, be a mystic. Mystical states of mind in every degree are shown by history, usually though not always, to make for the monistic view. . . . The paragon of all monistic systems is the Vedanta philosophy of Hindostan, and the paragon of Vedantist missionaries was the late Swami Vivekananda. (Lokeswarananda, 32)

Vivekananda was not only a paragon of Vedanta but also a paragon of Indian English literature. As V.K. Gokak puts it: "His writings on Bhakti-, Jnana-, Karma- and Raja-Yogas, on Advaita, on Practical Vedanta, on personal and impersonal Deity are classical documents in the field. It is difficult to find a mind closer to reality, more philosophic, more comprehensive and more modern than that of Swami Vivekananda."

Among these works, *Raja-Yoga* is his most assiduously composed work of art for which he managed several books from India. He dictated the whole book in his private classes. *Jnana-Yoga* comprises ten lectures delivered in London and six in America. The *Raja-Yoga* displays not only his descriptive power but also establishes him as a translator *par excellence.* His secretary Miss Sarah Ellan writes on his mode of writing: "In delivering his commentaries on the Sutras, he would leave me waiting while he entered deep states of meditation or self contemplation, to emerge therefrom with some luminous interpretation. I had always to keep the pen dipped in the ink. He might be absorbed for long periods of time and then suddenly his silence would be broken by some eager expression or some long deliberate teaching." (*Life*, 2: 60) He gives these a book form consisting of eight chapters in the first part and four chapters in the second part named *Patanjali's Yoga Aphorisms* with a Preface and an 'Appendix.' The second part is the translation of *Patanjali's Yoga Aphorisms*. The book, published in 1896 from New York, received appreciation from Leo Tolstoy.

The 'Preface' gives a historical account of Raja-Yoga as well as his plan of work in epigrammatic and pithy sentences: "It brings dependence; it brings fear; it brings superstition." (*Works*, 1: 129) The sentence structure not only in this context but elsewhere as well reminds us of Bacon's sentences but with less epigrammatic strength. The language is bereft of terminology, conceit, far-fetched metephors and ambiguities. The 'Preface' gives a glimpse of his prose style: "The second part is a rather free translation of the aphorisms of Patanjali, with a running commentary. Effort has been made to avoid technicalities as far as possible, and to keep to the free and easy style of conversation." (*Works*, 1: 122)

Though the style is simple and conversational, it is no less virile than his oratorical speeches. There is great difference between the two. The former draws its strength and energy from the bare honesty and simplicity of the language but the latter brings forth its cogency from the rhetorical devices, the ornate and the elaborate style so persuasive and pervasive. The prose of *Raja-Yoga* is like a scientific essay. Blended in it are the elements of expository, argumentative and philosophical style:

> What is the use of such knowledge? In the first place, knowledge itself is the highest reward of knowledge, and secondly there is also utility in it. It will take away all our misery. When by analyzing his own mind, man comes face to face, as it were, with something which is never destroyed, something which is, by its own nature. eternally pure and perfect, he will no more be miserable. no more unhappy. (*Works*, 1: 130)

The philosophy contained in the expository and argumentative prose is the highest ideal of Vedanta—the oneness of the cosmos.

Besides it, the passage is an example of hypertactic style that is common in Swamiji whenever he writes or speaks a longer sentence. His speeches, however, are not bereft of paratactic style as in this:

> As it were to give a living example of this preaching, as it were to make at least one part of it practical, the preacher himself came in another form, and this was Shakyamuni, the preacher to the poor and the miserable, he who rejected even the language of the gods to speak in the language of the people, so that he might reach the hearts of the people, he who gave up a throne to live with beggars, and the poor, and the downcast, he who pressed the pariah to his breast like a second Rama. (*Works*, 3: 263)

Clauses in this long periodical sentence are loose enough to fall apart.

Bhakti-Yoga and *Karma-Yoga* are the product of his class lectures delivered from December to February 1896. Surprisingly enough, none of the lectures of the beginners's class are included in his book *Bhakti-Yoga*. They are produced separately in Volume IV of *Complete Works*. The first part of *Bhakti-Yoga*, similar in substance to his beginners's classes, consists of articles written by him for the *Brahmavadin*. Marie Louise Burke reports: "It is in the 'Addresses,' therefore, that we find Swamiji's words as he spoke them directly to the students in his beginners' classes, scolding them at times for their intellectual scorn of an 'anthropomorphic' Personal God and at other times for running after psychic phenomena—ghosts and hobgoblins."

The two sets differ in language, style and effect. The language of the Addresses is simple, spoken, straightforward and devoid of abstractions and technical terms while the lessons for the beginners in the book *Bhakti-Yoga* are laden with Sanskrit quotations and terminologies. Otherwise the two sets are almost identical. We may well quote for illustration two identical passages, the first from the book and the second from the "Address":

> There are still greater dangers in regard to the transmitter,

> the Guru. There are many who, though immersed in ignorance, yet, in the pride of their hearts, fancy they know everything, and not only do not stop there, but offer to take others on their shoulders; and thus the blind leading the blind, both fall into the ditch.
>
> "Fools dwelling in darkness, wise in their own conceit, and puffed up with vain knowledge, go round and round staggering to and fro like blind men led by the blind." (Katha Up. I 11.5) The world is full of these. Everyone wants to be a teacher, every beggar wants to make a gift of a million dollars! Just as these beggars are ridiculous, so are these teachers. (*Works*, 3: 47)
>
> There are still more difficulties for the "transmitter." There are many who, though immersed in ignorance yet, in the pride of their hearts, think they know everything, and not only do not stop there, but offer to take others on their shoulders, and thus 'the blind leading the blind, they both fall into the ditch.' The world is full of these; everyone wants to be a teacher, every beggar wants to make a gift of a million dollars. Just as the latter is ridiculous, so are these teachers. (*Works*, 4: 23)

The word 'dangers' and the phrase 'in regard to' of the former's first sentence are replaced by 'difficulties' and 'for' in the latter which are more concrete and convincing. Again, the word 'think' in place of 'fancy' is more common. In the last sentence, the use of pronoun 'latter' is more appropriate. The latter does away with the quotation. The simplicity of the latter befits the beginners. The overall differences in the two texts are in nomenclature, classification, in the use of some prepositions, words and quotations. The former is better for the article than for the novice students.

The latter part of the *Bhakti-Yoga* entitled *Para-Bhakti* designed for the advanced course deservedly admits some Sanskrit quotations and phrases with their translation. A wonderful flow of love proceeds through each sentence: "We see love everywhere in nature. Whatever in society is good and great and sublime is the working out of that love." (*Works*, 3: 73) Love is identified with God and frequently personified. The frequent use of the word

'Love' is all too obvious. There is no fire of Sannyasin's spirit; it is all loving, emotive, calm and tranquil. There is no trace of rhetorical fire that one finds in many of his speeches. There is no irony, no invective, no sarcasm. It is emotive, devotional and to some extent mystic writings as against the psychological writings of *Raja-Yoga*. It draws heavily upon the *Gita* and the *Upanishads*. Swamiji finds the true embodiment of *Bhakti-Yoga* in Gopi's love for Krishna. But Swamiji perhaps fails to catch the wonderful love of *Vatsalya*, that one finds animated in the poetry of Sur Dasa. *Bhakti-Yoga* and *Vedanta* are the two subjects that have greater number of Sanskrit quotations and words written in Sanskrit language. This is peculiar about Swamiji's prose. We usually do not find this in Indian English writers though Latin and French expressions are common and are taken for the sign of scholarly and sublime writings. One plausible reason can be that he would not be at home in the art of Romanization, though he had done Romanization of words here and there. Another reason can be the fact that he took Sanskrit for a sign of grandiloquence and elegance and to make his style grand and sublime he might have experimented the use of Sanskrit in English as Latin and French are used. It is again typical of Indian preachers who cannot help using Sanskrit *Mantra* or *Sloka* in their oration. If it is his inability to do Romanization or translation, it shows both his diffidence and his honesty in his language. Take for example a typical Vivekananda style of sentence-making—It is (Abrahmani Brahmadrstya Anusandhanam). "Vedanta in All its phases" is another example of his grand style by means of images, similes, metaphors and Sanskrit quotations that he uses to elevate the style:

> Away back, where no recorded history, nay, not even the dim light of tradition, can penetrate, has been steadily shining the light, sometimes dimmed by external circumstances, at others effulgent, but undying and steady, shedding its lustre not only over India, but permeating the whole thought-world with its power, silent, unperceived, gentle, yet omnipotent, like the dew that falls in the morning, unseen and unnoticed, yet bringing into bloom the fairest roses. (*Works*, 3: 322)

The Ciceronian sentence structure consisting of simile 'dew' and symbols of 'roses,' 'light' and 'bloom' make it a piece of grand style. Marie Louise Burke's assessment is that it is a classic example of 'oratorical art.' A perusal of his speeches gives an impression that his language is simpler and sentences are shorter in his lectures in the West than in his speeches in India.

If the language of the *Bhakti-Yoga* is poetic, the language of the *Karma-Yoga* is prosaic and the prose didactic and moralistic; the language of the *Jnana-Yoga* is illustrative, repetitive and ornate and the prose highly philosophic. *Karma-Yoga* heavily draws on the teachings of the *Gita*. Swamiji does not appreciate the stand taken by Arjuna in the Kurukshetra and upholds Lord Krishna's rebuffing of his being a coward and hypocrite: "Arjuna became a coward at the sight of the mighty array against him." (*Works*, 1: 39)

Vivekananda was a moralist who preached non-attachment, non-resistance, selfless action and dutifulness. He reads from Maha-Nirvana-Tantra that prescribes a set of duties for all—the householder, the children, the women. To him, a *Karma-Yogi* should stick to his duty as Satan in Milton's *Paradise Lost* or Ravana in the *Ramayana* did. The central ideas of *Karma-Yoga* are driven home by parables and other stories. To illustrate the duty of a householder, he tells the story of birds who being the householders sacrificed themselves to feed the three guests—the King, the Sannyasin and the princes. Showing this, the Sannyasin narrates the duty of a householder to the king:

> King, you have seen that each is great in his own place. If you want to live in the world, live like those birds ready at any moment to sacrifice yourself for others. If you want to renounce the world, be like that young man to whom the most beautiful woman and a kingdom were as nothing. . . .
>
> Each is great in his own place, but the duty of the one is not the duty of the other. (*Works*, 1: 51)

The art of teaching here reminds us of the hermit in Leo Tolstoy's story "Three Questions" in which the hermit teaches the king in the same practical manner. Again, parables and fables have always been the favourites of the preacher, be it Christ, Buddha or Shri Ramakrishna.

Though Swamiji gives a systematic presentation of the succeeding stages in *Karma-Yoga* in a language that suits the subject and the preacher, its sentences are loosely connected and hence give the look of a loose style: 'We become lazy, we cannot move, we are inactive, bound down by certain ideas or by mere dullness." (*Works*, 1: 36)

The treatise of *Karma-Yoga* against that of *Bhakti-Yoga* rarely comprises direct quotation though it entombs allusions and references to wide ranging sources.

'The chief elements of style,' according to S.H. Burton, are 'diction, imagery, and rhythm.' An in-depth study of diction in a work of art is the work of a semantics, but even the briefest consideration will show Swamiji's mastery of English diction, his taste and his skill in the use of words. Though Swamiji was well read and had a sound knowledge of Bengali, Sanskrit, Hindi, Persian, Latin and French, and had browsed German and French literature, he rarely, if ever, used French, Latin and German words or expressions. His favourite French words that he used in his speeches and writings are *raison d'etre, reductio ad absurdum, deus ex machina, regressus ad infinitum, affaire d'amour, sine qua non*, etc.

It shows Swamiji's diffidence in the use of foreign expressions. He did not have a strong association with French and Latin expressions though he had written a few letters in French. And since his speeches and dictation were extempore, and since he did not pester himself for uncommon words, they did not come out naturally. His vocabulary is laden with Vedantic and scriptural terms which are confined to the Hindu scriptures and the *Bible*. So is the case with his quotations. There is dominance of Saxon words, Indian words and words drawn from everyday speech in his prose though he has employed skilfully words drawn from Latin and French origin and a wide range of images to give an air of immensity and magnificence. As a matter of fact, no absolute distinction can be made between the referential and the affective use of language. The difference is in degree. As an orator, he evokes emotion but also supplies factual information. The language of

Bhakti-Yoga is more affective than that of *Jnana-Yoga*. Even the pieces like "On Art." "On Language," "The Basis for Psychic or Spiritual Research," historical essays like "Aryans and Tamils" and objective essay like "Fundamentals of Religion" display the flavour of emotive language: "The attempt to make the Bengali language perfect in so short a time will make it cut and dried. . . . The greatest poet in Bengal was Kavikankana. The best prose in Sanskrit is Patanjali's *Mahabhashya*." (*Works*, 5: 259) The urge in these lines is emotive. In these articles, facts are directly stated, description depending little on imagery tends to be descriptive and the words are referential: "Again, although strictly speaking there are no absolutely racial religions, yet it may be said that, of this group, the Vedic, the Mosaic, and the Avestic religions are confined to the races to which they originally belonged." (*Works*, 4: 375)

Words like 'racial religions,' 'race,' 'Vedic,' 'Mosaic,' 'Avestic' are referential and connotative in suggestions rather than emotive. In most of his works whether they are emotive, narrative or descriptive, there is a directness of expression. Consciously or unconsciously, he might have imbibed directness of expression from J.S. Mill. Whenever he has to make clear and persuasive statement of ideas, he prefers the direct expression. There is no trace of difficult imagery without proper explanation as he himself says: "Simplicity is the secret. My ideal of language is my Master's language, most colloquial and yet most expressive. It must express the thought which is intended to be conveyed." (*Works*, 5: 259)

Like all great preachers Swamiji also made adroit use of figures of speech and images.

> The human mind is like that monkey, incessantly active by its own nature; then it becomes drunk with the wine of desire, thus increasing its turbulence. After desire takes possession comes the sting of the scorpion of jealousy at the success of others, and last of all the demon of pride enters the mind. (*Works*, 1: 174)

Whatever images, and symbols he employs are mostly concrete, descriptive and suggestive of his ideas:

> India will be raised, not with the power of the flesh, but with the power of spirit: not with the flag of destruction, but with the flag of peace and love, the garb of the sannyasin; not by the power of wealth, but by the power of the begging bowl. (*Works*, 4: 352)

It may be urged that there is what might be called 'fossilized imagery' in the text. They are not usually thought of as images or treated as such in criticism. Phrases like 'the garb of the *Sannyasin*, 'the begging bowl' and 'the flag' are connotative. The author wants to drive home the idea that the progress of India will spring from religion and not from matter. In the above quoted line, the balanced and parallel structure (not with . . . but with . . . not by the power . . . but by the power) develops a rhythmic pattern. Syntactical parallelism with phonological stress and pitch elements achieves a more subtle rhythmic effect. But this is a too obvious and outdated pattern. The twentieth century writer seems to rely less on syntactical repetitions and more on an interplay between a primary rhythm and a secondary rhythm. This is a sign of modernity in language that can also be found in Vivekananda's prose:

> From the high spiritual flights of the Vedanta philosophy, of which the latest discoveries of science seem like echoes, to the low ideas of idolatory with its multifarious mythology, the agnosticism of the Buddhists, and the atheism of the Jains, each and all have a place in the Hindu religion. (*Works*, 2: 6)

The stress pattern aptly indicates a metrical composition. The parallelism of construction, recognizably repeated, that was for so long the dominant feature of English prose rhythm is not much in evidence here as It is in the former quotation. The assonance of 'i' sound in 'high . . . flights,' 'ai' sound in 'ideas of idolatory' and the repetition of 'a' and ism'' in 'agnosticism' and 'atheism' and the repetition of 'i' sound and repeated use of possessive construction 'flights of Vedanta' are the rhythmic element that underline the sense and reinforce his emotion and feeling about the subject in the mind of the audience. They function as an aid to the clear communication of his discovery that each religion is true and each has its own place and value. This citation is from his "Paper on Hinduism" which is the first known article written by the Swami himself and it received great appreciation from the public and the critics.

As a true sannyasin, he can speak in the words of unforgettable poetic and spiritual power:

> May I be born again and again and suffer thousands of miseries so that I may worship the only God that exists, the only God I believe in, the sum total of all souls—and, above all, my God the wicked, my God the miserable, my God the poor of all races, of all species, is the special object of my worship.

The passage blends in itself the East and the West and spirituality and materialism. It is an excellent example of 'impassioned prose.' The conventional rhythm pattern here as elsewhere on his speeches is obvious. The second pattern of rhythm just delineated is the rhythm pattern that one often encounters in his prose writings. Thus we can safely submit that the Swami in his miscellaneous prose pieces in English numbering two dozen displays greater degree of modernity in language by virtue of precision, epigrammatic strength, rhythm pattern and compactness. They are by no means rhetorical. There is no repetition or contradiction. In language and style, they differ from his four books on Yoga. The style is not loose, nor the language conversational.

We have seen the directness of expression in Swamiji. But he can speak in another vein as well. Note the indirect expression in his emotive prose "Christ, the Messenger."

> The wave rises on the ocean, and there is a hollow. Again another wave rises, perhaps bigger than the former, to fall down again, similarly, again to rise driving onward. In the march of events, we notice the rise and fall, and we generally look towards the rise, forgetting the fall. But both are necessary, and both are great. (*Works*, 4: 138)

The passage in itself does not say anything but the image of 'wave,' 'ocean' and 'hollow' prepares the background in the light of which the life of Christ is dealt with in the succeeding pages. 'Ocean,' 'wave' and 'hollow' are the tenors that are suggestive of the 'rise' and 'fall' in the world of thought and religion. The chief purpose of these images is to show how 'hollow' that stands, for 'liberal ideas' are crushed by the 'wave' only to emerge like a phoenix with greater strength. The 'hollow' is a state, a predicament that can also be compared with demode state when Christ was born to cause a great 'wave'—Christianity.

Swamiji was equally good at narrative prose which shows his skill in dramatic exposition of character. Some narratives like "The Ramayana," "The Mahabharata," "The Story of Jada Bharata," "The Story of Prahlàda" "The Great Teacher of the World," "On Lord Buddha," "Christ, the Messenger," are in the tradition of Indian folk tale and the technique is that of the story telling of Indian priests and grandmother and grandfather. These narratives are full of dramatic exposition and short dialogues among the characters:

> Immediately, at the cottage was heard the voice of Rama, crying, "Oh, Lakshmana, come to my help!" and Sita said, "Lakshmana, go at once into the forest to help Rama!" "That is not Rama's voice," protested Lakshmana. (*Works*, 4: 69)

Swamiji presents the climax, crisis and the most sensitive part of the story in dialogue form that enlivens the story and helps to retain the dramatic effect of the original story. For example, the conversation between Savitri and Yamaraja in the story "Savitri and Satyavan" is presented in the dialogue form:

> He turned back "Savitri, daughter, why are you following me? This is the fate of all mortals." "I am not following thee, Father," replied Savitri, "but this is, also, the fate of woman, she follows where her love takes her, and the Eternal Law separates not loving man and faithful wife." Then said the God of Death, "Ask for any boon, except the life of your husband." "If thou art pleased to grant a boon, O Lord of Death, I ask that my father-in-law may be cured of his blindness and made happy." "Let thy pious wish be granted, du-

> teous daughter." And then the King of Death travelled on with the soul of Satyavan. Again the same footfall was heard from behind. He looked round. "Savitri, my daughter, you are still following me?" "Yes, my father; I cannot help doing so; I am trying all the time to go back, but the mind goes after my husband and the body follows. The soul has already gone, for in that soul is also mine; and when you take the soul, the body follows, does it not?" "Pleased am I with your words, fair Savitri. Ask yet another boon of me, but it must not be the life of your husband." "Let my father-in-law regain his lost wealth and kingdom, Father, if thou art pleased to grant another supplication." "Loving daughter," Yama answered, "this boon I now bestow; but return home, for living mortal cannot go with King Yama." And then Yama pursued his way. But Savitri, meek and faithful, still followed her departed husband. Yama again turned back. "Noble Savitri, follow not in hopeless woe," "I cannot choose but follow where thou takest my beloved one." "Then suppose, Savitri, that your husband was a sinner and has to go to hell. In that case goes Savitri with the one she loves?" "Glad am I to follow where he goes, be it life or death, heaven or hell," said the loving wife. "Blessed are your words, my child, pleased am I with you, ask yet another boon, but the dead come not to life again." "Since you so permit me, then, let the imperial line of my father-in-law be not destroyed; let his kingdom descend to Satyavan's sons." And then the God of Death smiled. "My daughter, thou shalt have thy desire now: here is the soul of thy husband, he shall live again." (*Works*, 4: 89)

The use of archaic words ('thou,' 'shalt,' 'thy,' 'thou art,' 'takest') and 'poetic construction ('Glad am I,' 'Blessed are your words') give weight, dignity and sonority to the narrative.

Among other narratives are sketches of some living personalities of his time who in one way or another had influenced him. These had been written by Swamiji in a narrative style but the sketches are bereft of dramatic quality. They are "On Dr. Paul Deussen," "On Professor Max Mueller," "Sketch of the Life of Pavhari Baba" and "My Master." They fall neither in the tradition of story telling nor in the tradition of biographical writings. They do not present the life of the subjects but rather present the character. Take for example his article "On Professor Max Mueller." It does not record his life, rather it presents the author's impressions about him. So the essay is impressionist rather than biographical. Here again, the typical Vivekananda admixture of English and Sanskrit in a sentence is to be found. "his *aparavidya* (lower knowledge) has indeed helped him to rich the *paravidya* (higher knowledge)." (*Works*, 4: 281) In these essays there is a periphrastic way of narration. Vivekananda does not come straight to the subject. See the opening lines of the "Sketch of the Life of Pavhari Baba."

> To help the suffering world was the gigantic task to which the Buddha gave prominence, brushing aside for the time being almost all other phases of religion; yet he had to spend years in self-searching to realize the great truth of the utter hollowness of clinging to a selfish individuality. (*Works*, 4: 283)

Writing on Pavhari Baba, he begins from Buddha and gradually comes down to the subject. This style serves the purpose of putting the subject in the great tradition of renunciators. Vivekananda cannot be objective while writing or speaking on these subjects. At one place he confesses that he cannot remain unaffected while speaking on Ramakrishna. His words and ideas in all such pieces, however near the truth, are born of his admiration or *Bhakti* for them.

But Vivekananda comes out as an objective critic in "A Study of Sankhya Philosophy," "Sankhya and Vedanta," "On Art" etc. He expounds the ideas contained in Sankhya philosophy, takes up each idea, deals it in the light of other and shows the merits and shortcomings of each point. The criticism of shortcoming is marked by understatement and humility of the language while the merits receive hyperbolic treatment.

> So far there is no objection. But if we ask the Sankhya the question, "Who created nature?"—the Sankhya says that the

> Purusha and the Prakriti are uncreate and omnipresent, and that of this purusha there is an infinite number. We shall have to controvert these propositions, and find a better solution, and by so doing we shall come to Advaitism. Our first objection is, how can there be these *two* infinities? Then our argument will be that the Sankhya is not a perfect generalization, and that we have not found in it a perfect solution. And then we shall see how the Vedantists grope out of all these difficulties and reach a perfect solution, yet all the glory really belongs to the Sankhya. (*Works*, 2: 452)

See how hyperbolic is his general comment on the Sankhya: "The Sankhya philosophy of Kapila was the first rational system that the world ever saw. . . . How wonderful his perceptions were, and if there is any proof required of the extraordinary power of the perception of Yogis, such men are the proof. They had no microscopes or telescopes. Yet how fine their perfection was, how perfect and wonderful their analysis of things!" (*Works*, 2: 445)

Swamiji, however, maintains an individual dialectical and cross-questioning approach to the subject. There is a gradual step-by-step progression of his logic that drives home each aspect of an idea of theory. The method of his logic is mainly inductive. Swamiji's prose, though fraught with his learning, wit and scholarship, has child-like simplicity of his personality. Hardly a technical term is left unexplained. He depends more on simple common place illustrations, ingenious analogies, parables and fables and concrete images and less on a plethora of textual quotations drawn from the authorities, on abstract images and on far-fetched comparisons.

So far as aphoristisc style is concerned, it is at its best in his incomplete works: "India's Message to the World," "Fundamentals of Religion," in his sayings and 'Inspired Talks.' and in other articles that he had written himself. Nowhere else he displays greater affinity with Bacon, the master of aphoristic style, in the terseness and brevity of language. "India's Message to the World" consists of forty two listed aphorisms by way of enlisting them in the syllabus. Again "The Social Conference Address" contains a number of paragraphs consisting of a single sentence.

> It seems God created the Brahmin, God created the Kshatriya, but who created the Sannyasin? (*Works*, 4: 305)
>
> But they have not learnt the modern method of self-advertisement. (*Works*, 4: 305)

We may quote a few examples from his "Inspired Talks":

> Know you are the Infinite, then fear must die. (*Works*, 7: 7)
>
> Love is beyond time and space, it is absolute. (*Works*, 7: 11)
>
> Conquer yourself, and the whole Universe is yours. (*Works*, 7: 32)
>
> Be beyond both freedom and bondage. We are Shiva, we are immortal knowledge beyond the senses. (*Works*, 7: 32)

These are some of the oft-quoted proverbs from his texts.

The aphorism does not merely perfect accepted wisdom, it is also a proper vehicle for new inquiry, for intellectual adventures. Vivekananda was unlike Hooker, Raleigh and Milton in that he was opposed to Ciceronian style. Naturally he then identified himself with the Senecan that had dethroned Ciceronian style in the second half of the 16th century. In place of long periodical sentences, he preferred pithy and short units. He, however, comes closer to later Bacon than to early Bacon. Aphorisms and epigrams give Vivekananda's essays a singular force and weight and are packed with striking formulas and practical wisdom. But being a preacher, he had to expand his ideas; his objective was to make others understand his thoughts, not just to jot down his random feelings on different subjects as was the case with Bacon. Obviously, he could not afford the same terseness, brevity and understatement that Bacon could. His sentences, unlike Bacon's, attain a musical cadence which is the saving grace of the best prose of Donne, Browne and Milton. Again, his prose is replete with the flashes of poetic fire that one finds in D.H. Lawrence's prose. K.R. Srinivasa Iyengar, acknowledging his contribution to Indian English prose, writes: "Vivekananda spoke and wrote so often and with such intensity of feeling that he could hardly find the time or be in the mood to pause and refine his sentences. The words gushed out as it were, and carried with them the native energy and impetuosity of his mind and his feeling for the common people. The many volumes of his English prose constitute part of India's cultural history, but he should be counted more among our prophets and builders than among mere masters of prose." (536)

The Swami had no time to revise or refine his sentences and yet his sentences rarely, if any, give pass to any error or flaw. This is a unique quality in itself. Of course, his sentences can be restructured but in most cases they will lose their oratorical effect. His prose written or spoken has to be judged from the *Arse Predicandi's* point of view. His prose in general is not a scientific essay that it calls for a very compact structure. His language is flexible and not pedantic. To illustrate the point, we may take an example: "It is a man-making religion that we want. It is a man-making education that we want. It is man-making theories that we want." (536) A modern writer will perhaps restructure it in this way. "It is the man-making religion, education, and theories that we want." It is of course compact and tightly structured sentence but it lacks rhetorical flare of the former.

We have proof enough to suggest that Vivekananda was conscious of style and was always conscious of the decorum. As he wrote to Alasinga about the magazine *Awakened India*:

> There is yet a vast untrodden field, namely—the writing of the lives and works of Tulasidas, Kabir, Nanak and of the saints of southern India. They should be written in a through going, scholarly style, and not in a slipshod, slovenly way. In fact the ideal of the paper, apart from the preaching of Vedanta, should be to make it a magazine of Indian research and scholarship, of course bearing on religion. (*Works*, 5: 116 Ep. LXVII)

And then again to Nanjunda Rao about the design of *Prabudha Bharata*: "A design should be simple, symbolical, and condensed. I will try to make a design for *Prabudha Bharata* in London and send it over to you." (*Works*, 5: 114, Ep. LXVI) He writes to Alasinga about the publication of *Jnana-Yoga* in *Awakened India*. "They have to be very carefully gone through and all repetitions and contradictions taken out. I am sure I will have more time to write." (*Works*, 5: 115-16, LXVII)

We know that *Jnana-Yoga* is the collection of his lectures and before letting it publish, he asked for the removal of repetitions and contradictions. This very fact dispels doubts, if any, about his mastery of written and spoken style. This awareness is noticeable in his writings. Despite paucity of time, he was conscious of style. His articles contributed to the *Metaphysical* magazine, New York, are quite scholarly. In them he makes a comprehensive study of the subject in world's perspective by interlarding them with specific references of and quotations from world thinkers. The language and style of these are best suited for a standard article. In his article "Reincarnation," for example:

> The ancient Hebrews never disturbed their equanimity by questioning themselves about the soul. With them death ended all. Karl Heckel justly says, "Though it is true that in the Old Testament, preceding the exile, the Hebrews distinguish a life-principle, different from the body, which is sometimes called 'Nephesh' or 'Ruakh,' or 'Neshama,' yet all these words correspond rather to the idea of breath than to that of spirit or soul. Also in the writings of the Palestinean Jews, after the exile, there is never made mention of an individual immortal soul, but always only of a life-breath emanating from God, which, after the body is dissolved, is reabsorbed into the divine 'Ruakh.' The ancient Egyptians and the Chaldeans had peculiar beliefs of their own about the soul; but their ideas about this living part after death must not be confused with those of the ancient Hindu, the Persian, the Greek or any other Aryan race. There was, from the earliest times, a broad distinction between the Aryas and the non-Sanskrit speaking Mlechchhas in the conception of the soul. Externally, it was typified by their disposal of the dead—the Mlechchhas mostly trying their best to *preserve* the dead-bodies either by careful burial or by the more elaborate processes of mummifying, and the Aryas generally burning their dead. Herein lies the key to a great secret—the fact that no Mlechchha race, whether Egyptian, Assyrian, or Babylonian, ever attained to the idea of the soul as a separate entity which

can live *independent* of the body, without the help of Aryas, especially of the Hindu." (*Works*, 4: 259)

Again, it is true that Vivekananda was one among the builders of Indian English prose that had its origin in Raja Rammohun Roy and was nurtured and developed by Keshub Chunder Sen, Ranade and Michael Madhusudan Dutt. Swamiji made a clear departure from the existing trend of English-educated young men of his time. The 'Derozio men,' as some of them are called, gave unrestrained expression to their 'excessive enthusiasm for things British and the excessive derogation of things Indian (or Hindu).' Swamiji, contrary to all this, reinterpreted India's past glory and spiritual heritage and established India's spiritual superiority over the West. Others used to sit at the feet of the West but Vivekananda made the West sit at his feet. The prose of that time was the result of political activities and thus has little literary and perennial value. Swamiji's prose has most of the literary qualities of a good prose. He introduced a systematic body of metaphysics and philosophy to Indian English literature, In fact, the whole of Hindu religion and philosophy was translated into English for the first time by an Indian monk. He enriched English language by introducing a panorama of new words, images, and expressions culled from the Hindu scriptures and some drawn from everyday life. *Mahat, Prana, Om Tat Sat, Tatha, Purusha, Prakriti, Tanmatras, Manas, Chitta, Vritti, Indriya, Buddhi, Linga Sharira, Jiva, Advaita, Akasha, Ida, Pingala, Sushumna* and *Maya* are some of them. His prose is more the depiction of nounmenon than that of phenomenon world that is the characteristic of his contemporaries. He broke away from the Macaulayan tradition and introduced a type of his own laden with the Hindu phraseology that makes his style more distinct than others and perhaps no one's style among his contemporaries is more characteristic of the age of Renaissance and more positive than his. The total output in a span of just nine years of his literary career is so voluminous, qualitative and varied in genre (Prose, Oratory, Poetry, translation, letters, travelogue) and in subjects that we cannot undermine his historical and literary value in the study of Indian English literature. But unfortunately, he had to receive much literary attention at the hands of critics which is certainly his due. Such a force he was in the world literature that literary stalwarts like Leo Tolstory, D.H. Lawrence, Aldous Huxley, Henry James and Christopher Isherwood were deeply influenced by his writings. R. Rybakov writes that reports of Swamiji's lectures in the newspaper "stirred the writer [Leo Tolstoy] profoundly and for a while he could not continue reading. He went to the bedroom and read Vivekananda's books all through the night." (63) Leo Tolstoy once remarked: "What English has Vivekananda! He has learnt all its subtleties." (34) It is relevant to quote Christopher Isherwood's comments on his art of speaking: "One of the most enchanting things about Vivekananda is the way he was eternally changing sides when he was speaking to different people; he could denounce the British in words of fire, but again he would turn on the Indians and say: 'You cannot manufacture one pin, and you dare to criticize the British!' And then he would speak of the awful materialism of the United States, and on the other hand, he would say that the treatment of women in India was absolutely disgraceful." (53)

It is the spirit of assimilation in him that finds beautiful expression in his prose. In it are assimilated the spirit of mysticism and socialism, the concept of the other world and that of this world, Vedanta and the concept of *Daridranarayana*, renunciation and social work, the seeds of revolution and internationalism sublimated. And at last this perusal comes to the conclusion that Vivekananda was a master and one of the pioneers of Indian English prose style who developed Indian English non-fictional prose and gave a wider perspective and a universal dimension to it.

Conclusion

The attempt to peruse Swami Vivekananda's writings and speeches from literary point of view has suffered badly because of his neutrality and much ado about his philosophic and religious feat. After such assaults, the Swami, the poet, the litterateur seems barely recognized and he has never tried to put himself in that way. A perusal of his letters explicitly reveals that he was interested in the art of writing and consciously a writer. Though like Gandhi he had to write or talk a great deal (often in English) even as we have to walk or eat or breathe: he wrote consciously a number of articles for *Metaphysical* magazine, *Awakened India, Brahamavadin*, a few incomplete books, four treatises on Yoga, some narratives—"Memoirs of European Travel," "The East and the West" and life sketches that were more than a routine work. They reveal his love for writing. We know how he longed for writing a book of stories on the pattern of *Alice in Wonderland*. One can approach these works from a literary perspective. This work is an attempt to show that a philosophic reading is perfectly compatible with a respect for artistry or literary study. Indeed, given the genesis of these works, such a reading is unavoidable for a philosophic literature for which the Swami stands next to none in Indian-English literature. It is also a critique of his oratory, prose, poems, and it measures his contribution to Indian-English literature. Implicit in my argument is the obsession of wild-eyed enthusiasts who seek to convert others to the faith that all religious and philosophic works must always be read from such a perspective. Such a notion is not born of a particular criticism but of the general indifference to the literary study of the Vivekananda's works. It is a bitter fact that there is hardly a book on the history of Indian-English literature that comprises an exclusive chapter on Vivekananda.

Here and there we find some stray remarks on this aspect or a few articles published in *Prabudha Bharata, Vedanta Keshari, Ramakrishna Mission Bulletin, Brahmavadin* or some pages in *Vivekananda O Samakalin Bharatavarsha, Chintanayak, Vivekananda* (the last two are comprehensive works in Bengali). Marie Louise Burke writes in her 'Author's Note': "Swamiji was, to be sure, a genius and a poet . . . his effort was always to benefit his listeners, never simply to give expression to his own inner fire and light." Indeed to Vivekananda the primary object of literature or art is to instruct, and delight is subservient to it. In his case delight is 'eternal bliss.' His literature is not an imitation of illusion as Plato believes but an embodiment of Truth itself as Aristotle upholds and Vivekananda maintains: 'the secret of Indian art is to represent the ideal.' In this respect Vivekananda falls more in the tradition of Indian art than in the Greek or Roman. Again Sister Nivedita, Romain Rolland, His Disciples, Isherwood, K.R. Srivnivasa Iyengar, M.K. Gandhi. V.K. Gokak and many others maintain that he was a writer and admit his contribution to Indian literature. But they barely seem sufficient to give him the right place in Indian-English literature that he duly deserves. Iyengar devotes two exclusive chapters to Gandhi namely "Mahatma Gandhi" and "Gandhi Literature" while he devotes barely a few pages to Vivekananda and that too in the general chapter by way of reference. What is attributed to Gandhi by Iyengar, say simple, 'bare and austere writing' and 'Art for life's sake' actually fall in the province of Vivekananda. 'Bare and austere' speeches and writings are the limitation of Gandhi. It is because he could not write in ornate, figurative and scholarly English. Much before Gandhi, Vivekananda discarded Macaulayan English and advocated the use of simple, serviceable but expressive English and he practised it. Of course, when the situation called for scholarly English and grand style, like a true artist he showed his mastery over it. In this way he established his command over both simple and elegant English maintaining always the principle of decorum. Gandhiji himself writes in a letter to Avinashilingam on 22 July 1941: "Surely Swami Vivekananda's writings need no introduction from any body. They make their own irresistible appeal." (Lokeshwarananda, 55)

Vivekananda was a great scholar and wrote both in scholarly English and in simple everyday English. Romain Rolland points out the difference. "But this difference will always remain between the thought of Gandhi and that of Vivekananda, that the latter, being a great intellectual which Gandhi is not in the slightest degree could not detach himself as Gandhi has done from systems of thought. While both recognised the validity of all religions, Vivekananda made this recognition an article of doctrine and a subject of instruction." (311)

Vivekananda, like Tolstoy and Gandhi, was not in agreement with the view that art or literature is purely autonomous and exclusive, and tried to make it a vehicle of his thought and 'a handmaid of life.' As he writes: "Now, true Art can be compared to a lily which springs from the ground, takes its nourishment from the ground, is in touch with the ground, and yet is quite high above it. So art must be in touch with nature—and wherever that touch is gone, Art degenerates—yet it must be above nature. Art is—representing the beautiful. There must be Art in everything." (V: 258-59) This makes it clear that any attempt to make purely literary evaluation of his works excluding his philosophy, theology and religion would be retarding and futile. One can no longer escape 'the fascination of the personality' and the universal appeal of his Advaita—the oneness of soul, the divinity of man and the unity of all religions.

Looked at from the literary angle, his literature can be placed in the tradition of Carlyle, Henry Newman, Herbert Spencer, John Ruskin etc. In England there has been a long chain of philosophical writers like them in all ages whose chief concerns were philosophy, theology and religion. They were studied in both disciplines—philosophy and literature. And there has always been men like Leslie Stephen who 'approached philosophy from the literary side.' Vivekananda took deep delight in the study of philosophical works specially those of Schopenhauer, Kant, Hegel, August Comte, J.S. Mill, Newman, Ruskin, Carlyle, Herbert Spencer, Max Mueller, and some others. In philosophy or religion, he barely comes under their influence. He accepts their ideas as far as they are in agreement with Vedantic thought. Though his boyish agnosticism was inspired by J.S. Mill, he subsequently overcame it by the training of his

Guru, Shri Ramakrishna, and emerged as an intellectual and mystical giant never to be bowed down by the personality of a writer, however great. He is appreciative of the German philosopher Schopenhauer for Schopenhauer is most appreciative of Vedantic religion. He quotes from Schopenhauer: "In the whole world there is no study so beneficial and so elevating as that of the Upanishads. It has been the solace of my life, it will be the solace of my death." (1990, 3: 109)

And Vivekananda perceives the permeation of Indian thought in the literature of the world. He echoes Kant in his concept of time, space and causation as the constituents of *Maya* but on the other hand improves upon him: "Kant has proved beyond all doubt that we cannot penetrate beyond the tremendous dead wall called reason. But that is the very first idea upon which all Indian thought takes its stand, and dares to seek, and succeeds in finding something higher than reason. . . . This is the value of the study of something that will take us beyond the world." (1990, 1: 199)

He comes closer to Carlyle than to J.S. Mill. Both were transcendentalist, idiosyncratic, authoritarian and in languages and style rhetorical. Mill, on the other hand, was empirical, reasonable and democratic. Mill has nothing of the Swamiji's 'rhetorical elan or imagination power.' We may illustrate the affinity between Carlyle's language and that of the Swami by quoting a passage from Carlyle: "Truly, if pressed to give definition, one might say this as soon as anything else: If your delineation be authentically *musical*, musical not in word only but in heart and substance, in all the thoughts and utterances of it, in the whole conception of it, then it will be poetical; if not, not-Musical; how much lies in that?" (Qtd. Daiches, IV: 956) Vivekananda time and again echoes such rhetorical style as in this: "If the Brahmin is he who has killed all selfishness and who lives and works to acquire and propagate wisdom and the power of love—If a country is altogether inhabited by such Brahimins, by men and women who are spiritual and moral and good, is it strange to think of that country as being above and beyond all law?" (1990, 3: 197)

His writings, here as elsewhere, are remarkable for their perspicuity and ease of style. Philosophy, in his pages, bears herself with grace as well as gravity. Vivekananda, like Carlyle, advocated renunciation, work and 'hero-worship.' But Vivekananda's 'hero' or 'divinities' are not the same as we find in Carlyle's *Heroes and Hero-Worship*. They are the prophet. the poet, the king and the like. In Vivekananda they are of two extremes—as Buddha and the downtrodden, *Daridaranarayana* 'Jiva as Shiva.' We can see how Carlyle's concept of work, 'work is worship,' 'all true work is Religion' in his book *Past and Present* finds an elaborate treatment in Vivekananda's *Karma-Yoga*. Again, both impose their own meaning on their choicest words—a meaning which leads them to the core of a favourite doctrine—by their rhetorical method of playing with it and repeating it. Carlyle in the above quoted passage imposes his own meaning on the word 'musical,' so does Vivekananda in a number of his choicest words—'Love,' 'Advaita,' 'fascination' 'Maya' 'renunciation' etc.

What is applicable to Newman in English literature seems applicable to Vivekananda in Indian-English literature. David Daiches maintains: "This phase of English religious history comes into the history of literature not only as part of the thought of many important men of letters but as part of the very fabric of the mind and art of at least one of the great Victorian writers—Newman himself." (4: 963)

Like Newman, Vivekananda's 'Addresses in the Parliament,' 'Addresses from Colombo to Almora,' miscellaneous speeches, theological and philosophical writings and his letters have their own interest—ethical, philosophical and literary. But his four treatises on Yoga have a status as literature in their own right in virtue of their quiet luminosity of style and the personal, persuasive and pervasive way in which he translated the whole of Hinduism—the thought of a perennial religion and developed system of philosophy—Advaita—of his own that harmonizes in itself Advaita and Vedanta, dualism, qualified monism and monism, the concept of *Daridranarayana* and that of Vedanta, religion and science and even materialism (in his own sense) and spiritualism. A literary critic would appreciate the way he interpreted abstract and abstruse philosophy of Hinduism in concrete and comprehensible terms and made it, for the first time, accessible to the world. Above all, in Truth doctrine, truth itself has the supreme value. Quoting *Sartor Resartus*, I.A. Richards writes in *Principles of Criticism*: "The infinite is made to blend itself with the finite, to stand visible, and, as it were, attainable there. Of this sort are all true works of art." (201) And 'of this sort' is the literature of Vivekananda and with him began a trend of mystic writing and an interest in metaphysics in Indian-English literature. Tagore and Aurobindo can be placed in that tradition.

A body of *Mantric* poetry that we find in Aurobindo was experimented by Vivekananda though on a very limited scale, for example, "A Hymn to the Divine Mother," "A Hymn to Shiva," "And let Shyama Dance There" (Bengali) or "Six Stanzas on Nirvana," "The Hymn of Creation" etc.

In general terms one might well put him in the tradition of Raja Rammohun Roy, K.C. Sen, Mahadev Govind Ranade and K.T. Telang, Derozio, for they all belong to the group of the Renaissance writers. Their writings are born of the British hegemony and the social, political, economic and religious milieu of the time. They all made an attempt to bring about a change in the society and to establish a close relation between the East and the West. We can see how K.C. Sen and Vivekananda echo each other in arrangement of ideas, eloquence, rhetorical wit and fire, in persuasiveness and forceful presentation of their ideas. See how Keshub tried to forge a link between India and England: "Let then India learn from England practical righteousness. Let England learn from India devotion, faith and prayer." (qtd. Iyengar, 44) But he can also speak with greater rhetorical power: "Behold the sweet angle of the East, into whose beauty the very colours of heaven seem to have been woven." (*Ibid.*)

However, Keshub is neither mystical nor Vedantic, nor is his language fraught with scriptural quotations, Sanskrit words and expressions like Vivekananda. John Wright writes about Vivekananda's style: "He had been brought up amidst polemics, and his habit of argument was mainly Socratic, beginning insidiously and simply by a story, or clear statement of some incontestable fact, and then from that deriving strange and unanswerable things. All through, his discourses abounded in picturesque illustration and beautiful legends." (1989, I: 407)

Though Vivekananda appreciates Michael Madhusudan's contribution to Bengali language, he makes a clear departure from

Madhusudan's unrestrained expression to his zeal for things British and from his verbal excess and excessive sentimentality. Iyengar rightly remarks that Madhusudan's speech is characteristic of 'the Age of Innocence; Vivekananda's speeches are the characteristic of the 'Age of Knowledge' or the 'Age of Experience.'

Like K.C. Sen, he was called 'a divine orator' and 'orator by birth' by the American press and was held in high esteem. J.L. Nehru maintains: "Rooted in the past and full of pride in India's heritage Vivekananda was yet modern in his approach to life's problems and was a kind of bridge between the past of India and her present. He was a powerful orator in Bengali and English and a graceful writer of Bengali prose and poetry." (1982, 336-37) One would, however, like to say that Swamiji was more an English writer than a Bengali one. Most of his works for which he is known are in English. Again, he wrote only seven poems in Bengali while twenty-five are in English.

As a prose writer, Radhakrishnan, Vinoba Bhave and Sister Nivedita may be called his true successors in Vedantic literature. Radhakrishnan's prose has the lucidity, clarity and simplicity of Vivekananda's prose but has greater epigrammatic strength: "Hinduism is a movement, not a position: a process, not a result, a growing tradition, not a fixed revolution."

A bulk of Vivekananda's literature constitutes of his extempore speeches; he spoke without any notes or preparation. But Radhakrishnan has nothing of the Swamiji's rhetorical flare and the fire of burning spirit to awaken India and to push her forward. Appeal-Avalanche reports: "He speaks English not only distinctly, but fluently, and his ideas, as new as sparkling, drop from his tongue in a perfectly bewildering overflow of ornamental language." (1990, 3:48)

Vivekananda can also speak straightforwardly in bare, unornamental language. "One thing I would tell you, and I do not mean any unkind criticism, you train and educate and clothe and pay men to do what?—To come over to my country and curse and abuse all my forefathers, my religion and my everything." (1989, I:462) This directness of speech, honest and bold expression can be found in the speeches of Mahatma Gandhi. But Nehru's prose displays greater compactness, brevity and epigrammatic strength. However,

Nehru's speech at the midnight of 15th August, 1947, "At the stroke of the midnight hour, when the world sleeps, India will awake to life and freedom" became a memorable classic like Vivekananda's Address at the Parliament of Religions: "Sisters and Brothers of America . . . ."

An interesting thing about Vivekananda is that he was not only concerned with religion and social work but was conscious of the problem of language, style and the standard of writing. Of course such writings are barely a few pages and cannot be called a critical treatise; but they are a result of his meditative thought. Such articles are: "On Art in India," "On Art," "On Language" and "The Bengali Language." He writes: "The language in which we naturally express ourselves, in which we communicate our anger, grief, or love, etc. there cannot be a fitter language than that . . . no artificial language can even have that force, and that brevity and expressiveness . . . as that spoken language. Language must be made like pure steel." (1990, 6: 187)

This becomes a pertinent comment on Vivekananda's own language and style though it was written for the Bengali magazine *Udbodhan* in the article "The Bengali Language." He was worried about the weaknesses in Bengali language, "properly speaking, it has no verbs" and advised to model it after Pali. He also criticized the hack writers who know nothing but to "crawl a few lines and get some fool to publish them." He also advised to maintain a scholarly style while writing on the lives of the great saints.

The basic difference between Vivekananda and other Indian-English prose writers like Nehru, Nirad C. Chaudhari and others is that the latter are meticulously painstaking about what they write whereas the former is intuitive and extempore even in writing. Vivekananda is nowhere concerned with the artificial style or with felicitous language; rather he seems to be concerned with the expressiveness of style and language. It is his personal experience of Truth, his zest for religious and social regeneration of India and intense passion for the humanity to weld the world together through his Advaita Vedanta that Vivekananda has communicated to his narrative and oratory. He preached the philosophy of the Advaita Vedanta and was convinced that only this could be the future religion of the world for it was inclusive, constructive and scientific besides its being essentially spiritual. His idea of cosmology, for example, comes close to that of science: "The universe has not been created by any extra-cosmic God, . . . it is self-creating, self-dissolving, self-manifesting." Further, the idea of the divinity of man, of the worship of living gods, the concept of mutual cooperation in all fields, the building of one world, nation building, and the concept of the Vedic God—'Infinite Knowledge, Infinite Bliss and Infinite Existence' are wonderfully relevant to every age and give his words the significance of the 'literature of permanence.' He wanted India to become a 'nation' with a European society and India's religion. He exhorted us to become 'an occidental of occidentals in your spirit of equality, freedom, work, and energy, and at the same time a Hindu to the very backbone in religious culture and instinct.' He had a message for both the East and the West and delivered it forcefully in words charged with poignant spirit of renaissance. He spoke on a good many things but his frequent injunctions were *abhay* (fearlessness) and 'strength,' 'weakness is death.'

His four treatises: *Raja-Yoga, Karma-Yoga, Bhakti-Yoga* and *Jnana-Yoga*, and his book on 'Practical Vedanta' were acknowledged as world classics and were highly praised by Leo Tolstoy. V.K. Gokak in an article professes: "His writing on Bhakti-, Jnana-, Karma- and Raja-Yogas, on Advaita, on Practical Vedanta, on Personal and Impersonal Deity are classic documents in the field. It is difficult to find a mind closer to reality, more philosophic, more comprehensive and more modern than that of Swami Vivekananda."

His contribution to Indian-English literature in particular and Indian literature in general is not confined to his lectures, Addresses and the four treatises; it extends to poetry also. Though his poetic out-put is not substantial, he is richly endowed with poetic sensibility. Though his poems are occasional, they are unified by the central theme of his Advaita Vedanta that leads to the development of a new tradition in English poetry. His spiritual creativity and mystical outpourings gave birth to a *Mantric* poetry that was later developed by Aurobindo. Like Aurobindo, his lyrical poetry is suffused with a philosophical and mystical glow which was new to Indian-English poetry. Much before Vivekananda, Derozio wrote English poems in sonnet form. Though Vivekananda as a poet cannot be placed in the tradition of Derozio or of his contemporaries Kashiprasad Ghose and Michael Madhusudan Dutt, there is a point of affinity between Derozio and Vivekananda. Both had an eye for Nature in its twin aspect of beauty as well as terror. This can be seen in Vivekananda's 'Kali the Mother.' Derozio writes in one of his sonnets:

> O Tyrant fate! thus shall I vanquish thee,
> For out of suffering shall I gather pleasure.
>
> (Qtd. Iyenger, 35)

Both Vivekananda and Derozio display the influence of the Romantics, but they differ in metre, form, diction and poetic credo. Vivekananda's poems, like his prose, give all the savour of Indian Renaissance, Vedantic ideology and catholicity, "its sense of heroism and martyrdom' in serene, calm and placid atmosphere. In a way, his poems present the optimism of the poet despite an air of pessimism, pain and mortification that hangs about his poetry. Despite his failure to give a definite form to his poetry and his weak control over metre, his poems appeal to our heart and conscience and leave us brooding. His poetry may be called the 'summing up' of his whole philosophy as it contains the gist of his teachings. V.K. Gokak, Saraswathi Gowrishankar and Akhauri Rajendra have deservedly appreciated his poetry in their articles. The present author sent a questionnaire to some eminent professors of English to know their view of Vivekananda's poetry. Their answers to the question, "Do you call his verse poetry?" may well be reproduced here. Dr. Ram Chandra Prasad's answer was "I will. I must." Dr. Visvanath Chatterjee opined: "He is certainly a poet but perhaps not of a very high order."

In poetic sensibility, in the richness of images, in appeal, in the spiritual and mystic creativity, Vivekananda is no less than any mystic poet. He arrives at a mystic union between man and God and successfully welds microcosm and macrocosm in his poems.

> "Thou art," "thou art" the Soul of souls
> In rushing stream of life.
> "Om tat Sat Om." Thou art my God.

My love, I am thine, I am thine. (*Works*, 7: 452)

This is a quotation from Vivekananda's poem sent to J.H. Wright in a letter that has not been included in the volume *Poems*. He also displayed his skill in translating Sanskrit poems into English verse. He was no less revealing in his Sanskrit and Bengali poems. Even in his prose, one can discover the poet behind the mask.

His letters like those of Nehru, Gandhi, Horace Walpole and Chesterfield deserve exclusive literary study. His letters, more often, carry the same message, the same Vedantic thought that one finds in his speeches and other writings. They are rather more literary, in a sense—they blend his personal accounts and the accounts of philosophy and religion. It is his philosophy and idealism that help him metamorphose the personal into impersonal and temporal into universal. They are more revealing of his personal characteristics.

His preoccupation with Hinduism is not a bar to his being a litterateur. Hindu literature, myth and philosophy have aroused refreshing interest in the Western writers, poets and philosophers. The Vedic religion, the Puranic stories, Upanishadic philosophy and classical literature of the Hindu and the Buddhist have provided rich nourishment to the creative urges or spiritual yearnings of the Western artists and thinkers. Sir William Jones, Colebrooke, Bournouf, Paul Deussen, Max Mueller and Rhys David contributed to the reawakening of interest in the past heritage of India. Harder, Goethe, Schiller, Schilling, Schopenhauer, Kant, Hegel, Fichte of Germany, Victor Hugo and Voltaire of France, Shakespeare, Chaucer, Langland, Donne, Blake, Wordsworth, Coleridge, Scott, Moore, Shelley, Keats, Browning, Tennyson, Carlyle and Yeats of England, Thoreau, Emerson and Walt Whitman of America have derived inspiration in varying degrees from the Hindu literature. If Schilling found 'the maturest wisdom of mankind' in the *Upanishads*, Schopenhauer found 'no study so beneficial and so elevating as that of the Upanisads' and Goethe's fascination for Kalidasa's *Shakuntala* led him to exclaim:

I name thee, O Shakuntala!
and all at once is said.

Hinduism is the fountain of India's strength, art and of everything as is Christianity for the Europe. Vivekananda says: "India is immortal if she persists in her search for God. But if she goes in for politics and social conflict, she will die." (Gambhirananda, 78) See how identical is T.S. Eliot's view: "If Christianity goes the whole of our culture goes." (1972: 122)

The literature written by Vivekananda has to be studied in the background of India's culture and religion. In him, we find a blend of history, philosophy, psychology, culture, religion and art of India together with personal agonies, bliss and autobiographical reminiscences. As Rabindranath Tagore said: "If you want to know India, study Vivekananda. In him everything is positive and nothing negative." (Lokeshwarananda, 34) If one wants to study Indian classical literature one cannot afford to miss Vivekananda.

Writing for him was not the *Sadhana* of Raja Rao, yet he was interested in it and there are a few works that can be called writing for writing sake. They are, for example, "Memoirs of European Travel," "The East and the West," "The Paris Congress of the History of Religions," "Modern India," etc. They were originally written in Bengali. They are descriptive prose and exhibit his writing skill. As he writes: "I owe you a description of the sea-voyage for seven days which will be full of poetry and interest, and be written in a polished, rhetorical style. (*Works*, 7: 298)

Vivekananda also spoke on Shakespeare, Milton, Homer and some other British poets but unfortunately the text is not available. As *Life* puts it: "Those in Madras who heard the Swami were amazed. This was the Vedas and Vedanta exhibited as science and at the same time brought to life in personal realization. Each day new gifts and areas of knowledge came to light. Today he would be speaking of Valmiki, Kalidasa and Bhavabhuti in almost the same breath as of Homer and Virgil, Shakespeare and Byron; tomorrow it would be of the Trojans and of the Pandavas, of Helen and of Draupadi. Now he would descant on the idealization of the sensuous in Greek art, and then would go on to contrast it with the whole Hindu art and culture towards the supersensuous." (I: 365)

The conclusion arrived at in the course of this study is that Vivekananda by the influences of Ramakrishna got transformed from his boyish atheism into a propounder of Advaita Vedanta and with this conviction produced volumes of work in the form of letters, speeches, prose-writings and poems which establish him as a prose-writer, letter-writer, orator and poet *par excellence*. He was a seminal mind in Indian-English literature who introduced a new trend in Indian literature—philosophic, mystic and Vedantic writings born of spiritual creativity—that kept Indian writers inspiring in one way or another and will keep doing so.

Bibliography

Works of Swami Vivekananda

The Complete Works of Swami Vivekananda. Calcutta: Advaita Ashrama, 1990. 8 vols.

The Nationalistic and Religious Lectures. Madras: Ramakrishna Math, 1990.

Philosophical and Religious Lectures. Madras: Ramakrishna Math, 1990.

Caste, Culture and Socialism. Almora: Advaita Ashrama, 1947.

Poem. Almora: Advaita Ashrama, 1947.

Critical Books

Abhedhananda, Swami. *Life beyond Death*. Calcutta: Ramakrishna Vedanta Math, 1947.

Athalye, D.V. *Neo-Hinduism*. D.H. Taraporewala & Sons, 1932.

Atkins, J.W. *Literary Criticism in Antiquity*. 2 vols. London: Methuen, 1952.

Basu, Sankari Prasad and Sunil Bihari Ghosh. *Vivekananda in Indian Newspapers, 1893-1902*. Calcutta: Dineshchandra Basu & Co., 1969.

Bowra, C.M. *The Romantic Imagination*. London: Oxford Paperbacks, 1961.

Brooks, Cleanth, and William K. Wimsatt. *Literary Criticism: A Short History*. Alfred A. Knopf, 1957.

Burke, Marie Louise. *Swami Vivekananda in the West: New Discoveries*. Calcutta: Advaita Ashrama, 1983.

Chakravarti, K.C., ed. *The Book of Job and the Gospel*. Calcutta: Booklore, 1982.

Chopra, P.N., B.N. Dury and M.N. Das, *A Social, Cultural and Economic History of India*. 3 vols. Macmillan, 1974.

Daiches, David. *A Critical History of English Literature*. Allied, 1985.

_____. *Critical Approaches to Literature*. Orient Longman, 1985.

Eliot, T.S. *Selected Essays*. London: Faber and Faber, 1951.

_____. *On Poetry and Poets*. London: Faber and Faber, 1957.

_____. *The Waste Land*. Macmillan, 1986.

Encyclopedia America. E.J .Arnold & Sons, 1969.

Facets of Vivekananda. Madras: Sri Ramakrishna Math, 1987.

Ford, Boris, ed. *A Pelican Guide to English Literature*. 3 vols. England: Penguin, 1970.

Gambhirananda, Swami, trans. *Aitaraya Upanishad* Calcutta: Advaita Ashrama, 1983.

_____. *Holy Mother Shri Sarada Devi*. Madras: Sri Ramakrishna Math, 1955.

Gandhi, M.K. *The Story of My Experiments with Truth*. Ahmedabad: Navjivan Publishing House, 1995.

Gupta, Mahendranath. *The Gospel of Sri Ramakrishna*. 2 vols. Madras: Shri Ramakrishna Math.

Humphreys, Christmas. *Zen: A Way of Life*. London: The English University Press.

Isherwood, Christopher, ed. *Vedanta for the Western World*. London: George Allen and Unwin, 1951.

_____. *Vedanta for Modern Man*. London: George Allen and Unwin.

Iyengar, K.R. Srinivasa. *Indian Writing in English*. New Delhi: Sterling, 1982.

Iyer, B.R. Rajan, *Rambles in Vedanta*. Calcutta: S.P. League, 1946.

Iyer, M.K. Venkatarama. *Advaita Vedanta, According to Samskara*. New York: Asia, 1964.

Jack, Ian. *The Poet and His Audiences*. Cambridge: Paperback Library, 1984.

Kaviraj, Gopinath. *Aspects of Indian Thought*. Burdwan: University of Burdwan, 1984.

Kouwenhoven, John, ed. *Leaves of Grass by Walt Whitman*. New York: Modern Library, 1950.

Leavis, F.R. *New Bearings in English Poetry*. Penguin, 1980.

The Life of Swami Vivekananda by His Eastern and Western Disciples. Calcutta: Advaita Ashrama, 1989.

Lokeswarananda, ed. *World Thinkers on Ramakrishna-Vivekananda*. Calcutta: Swami Ramakrishna Mission Institute of Culture, 1983.

Lucas, D.W. *Aristotle: Poetics*.

Memoirs of Ramakrishna. Calcutta: Ramakrishna Vedanta Math.

Monier, Williams. *Indian Drama*. Varanasi: Chowkhamba Series, 1963.

Murry, J. Middleton. *The Problem of Style*.

Nikhilananda, Swami. *Vivekananda: A Biography*. Calcutta: Advaita Ashrama, 1987.

Nivedita, Sister. *The Master as I Saw Him*. Calcutta: Udbodhan Office, 1918.

Palgrave, F.T., ed. *The Golden Treasury*. London: Oxford University Press, 1968.

Prabhavananda, Swami. *Patanjali's Yoga Sutras*. Madras: Sri Ramakrishna Math, 1990.

Prasad, Ram Chandra. *The Mystic of Feeling*. Delhi: Motilal Banarasidass, 1978.

Radhakrishnan, S. *The Brahma Sutra: The Philosophy of Spiritual Life*. London: George Allen and Unwin, 1960.

Rajneesh, Shri. *Meeting the Ultimate*. Pocket Books, 1990.

Ranganathananda, Swami. *Swami Vivekananda, His Humanism*. Moscow, University Lecture. Advaita Ashrama, 1983.

Richards, I.A. *Principles of Literary Criticism*. New Delhi: UBS, 1991.

_____. *Practical Criticism*. Allied, 1987.

Rodwell, J.M., Trans. *The Koran*. London and Melbourne: Everyman's Library, 1983.

Rolland, Romain. *The Life of Vivekananda and the Universal Gospel*. Trans. E.F. Malcolm-Smith. Calcutta; Advaita Ashrama, 1988.

_____. *Life of Sri Ramakrishna*. Calcutta: Advaita Ashrama, 1988.

Sampson, George. *The Concise Cambridge History of English Literature*. Cambridge: ELBS, 1970.

Samullyn, Arthur, et al, ed. *Introduction of Philosophy*. New Delhi: Prentice-Hall of India, 1967.

Sarma, D.S. *Renascent Hinduism*. Bombay: Bharatiya Vidya Bhavan, 1966.

Scott-James, R.A. *The Making of Literature*. New Delhi: Allied, 1984.

Sen, Gautam. *The Mind of Swami Vivekananda: An Anthology and a Study*. Bombay: Jaico, 1990.

Shakespeare, William. *King Lear*. Delhi: Oxford University Press, 1985.

Shaw, G.B. *Man and Superman*. Delhi: Surjeet, 1984.

Sinha, K.N., ed. *Indian Writing in English*. New Delhi: Heritage, 1979.

Sister Nivedita's Lectures and Writings. Calcutta: Nivedita Girl's School.

Pamphlets

Address on Vedanta Philosophy by Swami Vivekananda: The Ideal of a Universal Religion (Jan. 1896). New York.

Vedanta Philosophy: Lecture by Swami Vivekananda on "The Cosmos" (Jan. 1896). New York.

Vedanta Philosophy: Lecture by Swami Vivekananda on "The Atman" (Feb. 1896). New York.

Vedanta Philosophy: Lecture by Swami Vivekananda on "Bhakti Yoga" (Feb. 1896). New York.

Lecture by Swami Vivekananda on "The Real and the Apparent Man" (Feb. 1896). New York.

Journals

Prabuddha Bharata. Calcutta: Advaita Ashrama.

Vedanta Keshari. Madras: Ramakrishna Math.

Bulletin of the Ramakrishna Mission Institute of Culture. Calcutta.

Narottom: The Centenary of Vivekananda's Bharata Parikarma and Appearance in the Chicago Parliament of Religions. Ramakrishna Mission School, Narottem Nagar, Arunachal Pradesh, 1993)

The Indian Journal of English Studies. New Delhi: Orient Language, 1971.

Self-Realization by Paramahansa Yogananda. Vol. 63, No. 4, Fall 1992.

